*Writers of Wales*

---

Editors
MEIC STEPHENS     R. BRINLEY JONES

*T. Robin Chapman*

# ISLWYN
# FFOWC ELIS

University of Wales Press

Cardiff 2000

# I

*Literature is often greater when it is a handmaiden than when it is a mistress. At such times it lacks presumption, and has conviction, and it earns immortality for itself by claiming immortality for its message. For a writer who consciously uses his talent to promote his religion, or his nationalism, or his humanism, nothing but the best will do . . . I would be grateful for the Great Novel if it appeared, but I would be more thankful still for a steady stream of readable novels which arrest and amuse, have tidy storylines and evident craftsmanship. Not rubbish either. But the ordinary literature which is the daily bread of every nation not suffering from the megalomania of national servility.*

Islwyn Ffowc Elis has built a reputation on paradox. He wrote these words in 1957, in the same year, coincidentally, that the OXFORD ENGLISH DICTIONARY first recognized the phrase 'angry young man'. He was thirty-two years old, with seven years as a Presbyterian minister behind him, and had recently embarked on what was to be the first of two precarious spells as a full-time author and broadcaster in Welsh. Over the previous five years he had produced what was already a substantial body of popular fiction. His immediate audience in the first issue of the now defunct magazine, YR ARLOESWR, where the words appeared, was the estimated twelve to fifteen writers in Wales – the majority under thirty, he suspected – who had the raw talent to do the same. Between them, he predicted, Welsh literature could add another dozen novels a year to the canon.

If it seems a rather pathetic aspiration, at the end of the 1950s it could be regarded as relatively optimistic. The wider Wales he addressed, he later commented, was little more than a western extremity of England. It had no Welsh Office, no Secretary of State, Welsh Books Council or Welsh Academy, nursery-school movement nor a single Welsh-medium secondary school. It had no independent television channel, the Welsh Language Society had yet to be formed, and Plaid Cymru's first Westminster success was nearly a decade away. The 1951 Census had shown a decline of 200,000 in the number of Welsh-speakers over the previous twenty years. He could have added rural depopulation to his list, along with the decline of organized religion and falling readership of Welsh periodicals. For a young man of nationalist sensibilities there was plenty to be angry about.

This monograph is a study of two literary personalities. On the one hand there is Islwyn Ffowc Elis the genre-bender, the man who has experimented with comedies of manners, family saga, science fiction, farce and downright good reads. He has earned a reputation in Welsh literature unparalleled since the time of Daniel Owen at the end of the nineteenth century, as a serious literary figure who can be – and has been – read purely for pleasure. The literary landscape of the late twentieth century is inconceivable without him.

On the other, there is the *engagé* Islwyn Ffowc Elis, the committed writer for whom literature must serve a purpose outside itself. It is a belief which compels the critic to approach him as essentially a political animal and makes comparisons with the majority of writers of popular English-language fiction impossible.

*I write not necessarily what I want to write*, he famously said in a 1971 English essay, *but what is expected of some writers, at least, at this particular hour of the nation's history.* Today, it reads as a very direct, some would say a very Welsh, statement. In 1957, however, it challenged a critical orthodoxy which believed in 'Art for Art's sake' and dismissed the notion of popular, let alone committed, writing in Welsh as at best irrelevant, at worst a form of cultural prostitution. T. H. Parry-Williams wrote that the only duty of the writer was to entertain; Kate Roberts defended her decision to keep her novels and short stories free from political nationalism; Saunders Lewis dismissed the work of Islwyn Ffowc Elis's literary hero, Tegla Davies, as tainted with *the mildew of evangelicalism*. It would be twenty-five years before Islwyn Ffowc Elis could claim that *the wheel has turned and the committed writer has come into his kingdom.*

His story, then, is of a commitment to commitment, of a conviction which led him to become arguably the first writer since the days of the Court Poets in the sixteenth century to attempt to earn a living by writing in Welsh. At different times he has spoken of the need to write as duty, therapy and destiny, on more than one occasion warning would-be authors to avoid the call if they possibly can. Whether an urge to write which is not primarily a literary one compromises a writer's integrity is a question which must be explored. Can literature be regarded simultaneously as a commodity and a clarion call? Certainly, when conscience is coupled with a desire to entertain it makes for an interesting mix. Add the ingredients of inheritance, upbringing, personal taste and a world-view shaped by a very particular kind of Welshness, career fluctuations and wider concerns, and the recipe is all the more complex. It is a tribute to the man's principle or sheer bloody-mindedness that the intervening years have done nothing to alter his belief in either the dignity of popular fiction or in the artistic self-discipline of writing from an engaged perspective.

Islwyn Ffowc Elis was born Islwyn Foulkes Ellis at his aunt's council house in Wrexham, 12 The Beeches, Acton, on 17 November 1924. His name was taken from a volume of the collected works of the nineteenth-century mystic poet, Islwyn, which stood on a shelf in the corner. According to family tradition, his father greeted his first-born with the words, *I don't care what else he becomes as long as he is a poet.*

He was raised first in Glynceiriog and then, from the age of five, at the family farm, Aberwiel, outside the village. His home and immediate environs were thoroughly Welsh; less than two miles to the east lay the border with England. *For me, at quite an early age,* he wrote in the 1971 essay, *it had become not a border but a frontier:*

*We in our mountain valley spoke Welsh. They on the plain spoke English. We could sing spontaneously in harmony. They could not. We talked of preachers and poets, they of footballers and racehorses. As a boy, I was fascinated by the difference. As an adolescent, I was disturbed by it.*

The sentences above are a reminder of the caution

required when dealing with Islwyn Ffowc Elis's own account of his childhood. He is, after all, a creative artist. The Edwardian patriot O. M. Edwards wrote that when he saw snowflakes as a young boy, he believed that he was seeing bees in clean new clothes: a statement which Saunders Lewis was quick to pounce upon as a conceit derived from reading Dafydd ap Gwilym rather than from genuine memory. One suspects that something of the sort is going on here. Islwyn Ffowc Elis's talk of fascination with the English shading into unease and the equation of Welshness with chapel and Englishness with the betting shop is too syntactically balanced, and too neat, too easy, too all-embracing an explanation of his motives as a writer to make reliable material for even a short biographical sketch like this. There is a sense that it is either a division imposed by the author himself, or the reworking of a learned response.

This consciousness of border as a line of moral demarcation is, however, both genuine and significant. He told one interviewer in 1973:

*To be brought up in the aroma of Welsh culture, among Welsh books, and in a family which pursued literature, and particularly poetry, as a normal and praiseworthy thing – and almost on the border with England – this, above all, I am sure, made me what I am.*

The majority of his literary contemporaries either grew up in an environment where the English were summer visitors, or in the industrial south where English was a language spoken with a similar Welsh accent to one's own by the people next door. For

Islwyn Ffowc Elis in his particular corner of Wales, the English occupied their own space, the Welsh theirs, and consciousness of their presence was both immediate and distinct.

It is a mark of the Welshness of Glynceiriog in the 1920s and 1930s that Islwyn Ffowc Elis's mother, a non-Welsh-speaker from Ruabon, learned the language within a few years of marriage and spoke it consistently with the young Islwyn and his brother, Bryn. At the age of seven his knowledge of English was only passive. He has written of himself as *a weakly child . . . Not much of a player, no great shakes at kicking a ball*. His preferred games, it seems, were those which allowed him to impose a narrative on an imagination shaped by adventure stories, *seeing myself as a hero and a terror to uncivilized tribes, a captain of ships shooting lions by the score*. The language of this solitary play was English: *The outposts of the British Empire were the outposts of my dreams*. Welsh literary influences were more introspective still. The lyrics of Eifion Wyn, *my first and fullest love*, were models of poetry as refined observation simply expressed and of the poet as unintellectual, sensitive and attuned to nature. Eifion Wyn's TELYNEGION MAES A MÔR (*Lyrics of Field and Sea*), hugely popular in their time, were the perfect running commentary on the one-and-a-half-mile walk to and from school at Nantyr.

Primary school, in a one-room building with fifteen or so pupils and one mistress, left little impression upon him. He recited the lyrics of Ceiriog and developed a passion for sketching in pencil. Grammar school in Llangollen, which he attended between 1936 and 1942, was a different matter. Life there was lived *in terror of teachers and bullies.* The physical strain of travelling twenty-six miles daily was not eased by an anti-Welsh atmosphere within the school. When fellow-pupils learned of his nationalist sympathies, he was pushed into a wastepaper basket. He has more than once expressed indignation that he received no systematic grounding in Welsh history. Moreover, the areas in which he excelled or took a keen interest – scripture, music and art – were not examination subjects. Islwyn Ffowc Elis's defence was academic self-discipline – he took four Higher Certificates instead of the normal three and set his sights on the Methodist ministry, sitting additional papers on Old and New Testament scripture at around the same time. He undoubtedly worked too hard. When he left for university at Bangor in the autumn of 1942, he reminisced fifty years later, *the shackles were broken, and my feet were completely free for the first time ever.*

The first in his family to receive higher education, Islwyn Ffowc Elis was intoxicated and transformed by Bangor. *There were never, and never will be days like them,* he wrote in 1951, conscious even then that they were gone for ever. After the earnest endeavour of grammar school, Islwyn Ffowc Elis's years there were a glorious, thrilling waste of time. He would look back on the years between 1942 and 1946 as a period when his literature first had an audience.

*I wrote poetry and essays and short stories and worked with a variety of societies and staged reviews and sang in them and acted.*

In 1944 he won the Crown at the University of Wales Inter-College Eisteddfod. There was, too, a dizzy camaraderie which transformed the days of war in Bangor into something akin to a battle for the life of Wales. Bangor gave Islwyn Ffowc Elis a sense of Welshness as a shared experience and a consciousness that to be Welsh needed a degree of assertiveness, of carefree heroism, of exclusivity, which the English could never appreciate:

*The number of students was small, and half of them were tall and noisy Englishmen. It was a crisis for Welsh life; that crisis entered our veins and tied us closer together. Never was there such singing, no, even by the nightingales of the Rhondda, as our sporadic song on the day of judgment. We would come together in excitable clumps, and the song would rise from the depths of some lone tenor or pure soprano, and would swell until it mesmerized everyone. In the blind streets of the blackout, on the mornings of skipped lectures, everywhere – the song which kept Wales alive in every college stone. And when we scrimmaged and gathered, and the song rose into an exultation, the English around us would fall silent and dumb. Some with admiration, some with a sneer, but all of them dumb. Some kind of deference in the face of the song which made Wales Wales.*

Islwyn Ffowc Elis joined Plaid Cymru in the same year that he went to university. Although not instinctively a party man, his engagement with constitutional nationalism has been unwavering. In 1951, he briefly took on the editorship of the party's Welsh-language monthly, Y DDRAIG GOCH, served on its executive in the late 1950s and early 1960s and even fought two elections in the Liberal stronghold of Montgomeryshire in 1962 and 1964. His political triumph came, fittingly, as a writer – acting as press and publications officer for Gwynfor Evans in the Carmarthen by-election of 1966 which gave the party its first Westminster seat.

Academically, Islwyn Ffowc Elis's years at Bangor were a lost opportunity. His liberal education, what he knew of world literature, the arts and modern foreign languages, would, he later asserted, be self-taught. *I have come to the conclusion*, he says not completely without bitterness in the 1971 essay, *that, lacking worldly ambition as I did, 'education' was not designed for the likes of me.* He left with an undistinguished degree in Welsh and Philosophy and, after two years at the Theological College in Aberystwyth, where he gained a (much more creditable) BD, and a year's pre-ordination training in Bala, he followed his father's ambition for him to be a Methodist minister. He believes in retrospect that the expectation of others had conditioned him to a career for which he had no particular love or aptitude and that he was not brave enough, *or sure enough in my own mind to act independently.*

Married to Eirlys in 1950, he took a post in Llanfair Caereinion in the same year, turning down a *safe* (his italics) job with the BBC. It was a disaster. After the sociability of college life, he found himself exiled to a corner of Montgomeryshire which he did not know. He was to comment later that the move to Powys was like stepping back in time. He found the community in which he worked socially stratified in a way which was foreign to him (an experience which he was to use to effect in his early novels) and himself intellectually unchallenged, agonizingly *lonely and awkwardly unsuited to the work*:

*It became obvious to me very soon that I did not have a minister's temperament. I was too unsociable and I hated visiting houses to make small talk; my sermons were lessons rather than high-sounding perorations (to the alarm of the older members of the congregation), and attending regional committees and meetings and monthly meetings and conferences was a torment. I began to write more prolifically than I had done even at school and college, but that did nothing to lessen the pain. I tried a change of area, and moved to Newborough in Anglesey, but things were no better. The harness of the conventional ministry was too painful for this colt of a writer, and my health suffered.*

His unease with the ministry was signalled in a series of three dark pieces for the denomination's magazine, Y DRYSORFA, in 1955. They were the immoderate words of a man in despair. He questioned the contemporary relevance of the church, criticized its constitution and alluded strongly to his own unsuitability to continue within it. He proposed the closure of all chapels and churches for twenty years in favour of house meetings, questioned the whole basis of denominationalism, and argued that any sense of allegiance to the church was *no more than the instinctive attachment of human nature to what is familiar and customary.* His most telling criticism, however, had his own conscience at its heart:

*ministers don't write and lecture and broadcast and take classes just to increase their income, but because they find some self-expression in those tasks which they don't find in the ministry. To speak plainly, there is very little self-expression possible in today's ministry for a man with any modicum of talent. Today's ministers are not the same as yesterday's, but nor are the flocks. Nor the fold, nor the weather, nor the pastures.*

*Conscience,* Islwyn Ffowc Elis had the estimable Dr King say in BLAS Y CYNFYD two years later, *is responsible for more illness than we know.* Stress would be a theme in his fiction from then on, coupled closely always with a sense of unfulfilled duty.

He eventually left the ministry in 1956, filled with a feeling of *utter failure*. He moved back to Bangor and began working as a full-time broadcaster and writer, supplementing his income with part-time lecturing and extra-mural classes. While it lasted, it was a relatively comfortable existence. *Apart from my college days*, he recalled in 1973, *they were the most pleasant days of my life.*

The uncertainty of making a living and the responsibility of a daughter, Siân, born in 1960, led Islwyn Ffowc Elis to accept a lectureship at Trinity College, Carmarthen, in 1963. He stayed in the post for five years. It introduced him to the south, to a dialect of Welsh which he later added to his repertoire alongside those of Powys and Gwynedd, and a whole new network of friendships. The move brought with it, however, an end to his productivity as a writer. Islwyn Ffowc Elis has variously attributed *the drying of the creative faculty* to moving away from the company of mountains, to an increasing concern with nationalist politics and, simply, to having *written too much*. There is certainly some reason to believe the latter. In addition to his seven published books he had written *an unbroken stream* of material: plays and serials and musicals for radio and television, documentary scripts, talks, stage plays and scores of songs, articles, reviews and all sorts of other 'scribblings'. He has since expressed gratitude that his career was not aided or impeded by the arrival of a Welsh-language television channel which would have made it virtually impossible for him to concentrate on written fiction.

Paradoxically, too, in a secure post, the 'periodic neurosis' which provided the 'necessary tension' for his writing was lacking. It would be five years before Islwyn Ffowc Elis would attempt another full-length piece of fiction. There was a genuine commitment to academic life, too. Students from his days in Carmarthen, and later in Lampeter, describe him as a conscientious, often inspired teacher, in his element teaching the craft of creative writing and encouraging young talent. As a lecturer he admits an intolerance of idleness: a belated and vicarious atonement, perhaps, for his time in Bangor.

Islwyn Ffowc Elis took a job with the Welsh Books Council in 1968, working as director of a translation project. It gave him a chance to make use of his relative fluency in French, Italian and German, and he enjoyed the day-to-day work of editing, administration and corresponding with authors. He sensed throughout, however, that he was not really suited to the post, and in 1971 he began another spell as a freelance, based first in Carmarthen and later in Wrexham. Speaking in 1973, he described this second period of professional commitment as *a further challenge to philistinism*, an act of assertion that any country with pretence to culture should feel an obligation to support her writers. Welsh Books Council and Welsh Arts Council grants helped, but things were not so easy this time, and in 1975 he accepted the lectureship in Lampeter which he was to hold until his retirement in 1990. The University awarded him an Honorary D.Litt. in 1993, as much for his encouragement to young authors as for his own prolific output. He still lives in the market town with its small, arts-only academic community, in a bungalow with a view over open fields.

For someone who has lived such an itinerant existence, with five distinct careers, and homes in north, west and mid-Wales, Islwyn Ffowc Elis's belief in the value of belonging is arresting. Writing of the message of his fiction, he has said:

*It is that a man needs to belong – to a* patria, *be that defined as a neighbourhood or as a small nation-state (which I believe Wales should be), to a community, be it as small as a family or as numerous as a nation (which Wales is), to a creed-bearing movement, be it religious or political or whatever and/or to God. A man must feel and know that he belongs, and derive comfort and security from that assurance.*

Elsewhere, in a poem written in the late 1950s, 'Perthyn' (*Belonging*), now a staple of eisteddfod recitations, Islwyn Ffowc Elis expands on the mutuality of the idea, describing a sense of belonging as this atom-free totality:

*Rydw i gartre. Dyna'r unig ffordd o'i ddweud.*
*Rydw i'n perthyn i'r popeth di-ri'*
*Sy'n cydio amdana' i'n dynn, ac mae hwythau*
*Yn symud a bod ynof fi.*

(I am at home. That's the only way to say it.
I belong to the numberless everything
Which laps around me tightly, and they
Move and live in me.)

Writers a generation earlier tended to speak of belonging to Wales as a penance which was to be nobly borne. T. H. Parry-Williams, for example, wrote that there was no escape from the torture of Welsh identity; Prosser Rhys undertook to embrace her stigma and woe; Gwenallt variously likened her

13

to a grinning prostitute to be saved Gladstone-like from the clutches of English lust, and to ground consecrated by the dust of martyrs; Saunders Lewis spoke of Wales as a vineyard vouchsafed into his keeping. For Islwyn Ffowc Elis, as both man and author, any sense of self-sacrifice or moral obligation inherent in identity is tempered by a desire to embrace that identity: Wales is offered as much as it is imposed. It is, in a striking English phrase from the 1971 interview, *a continuing womb*, the only place where someone can feel fully human. In his fiction, then, the geographical and the social necessarily have a moral dimension. His stories are full of places where belonging defines the individual: a co-operative farm, the confines of a spaceship, as one of a crew of white workers in Black Africa, a branch of Plaid Cymru, a perfect society in the future. Small wonder, then, that so much of his fiction has at its heart the twin obsessions of exile and return, dislocation and deliverance, divorce and reconciliation, informed always by an ironic awareness that what has been lost cannot be appreciated until (sometimes too late) it has already gone. Islwyn Ffowc Elis's most interesting protagonists live at the end of a length of moral elastic stretched to, and beyond, breaking point.

Islwyn Ffowc Elis has never felt particularly at ease with the literary establishment and writes about critics of his own work with an endearing peevishness. He has described himself as *unashamedly popular* and *deceptively readable*, defending his decision to write as he does on three counts. He has argued that the ability to weave intricate plots (and his plotting is a definite strength) is dismissed largely by those who lack the ability themselves;

second, that writers of the standing of Joyce and Dickens have not been shy to write popular entertainments; and third, that popularity and profundity are not mutually exclusive. Writing of the last of these, he has said:

*Of this I am now fairly confident, though the boast will be despised. Posterity – that undying hope of all writers – will sift the trivialities in my work from the profundities, will lay aside the dross with tolerance and handle what silver remains with some affection.*

In a sense, time – the commodity which he has guarded most jealously – has justified him. As the raw contemporary material of his novels has metamorphosed into social history, his Wales of Woleseys and duffle-coats and political radicalism has assumed a moral universality. His characters engage and entertain us; more interestingly, they also make us think. Islwyn Ffowc Elis has become, retrospectively, both a chronicler and a novelist of ideas. His most successful fiction fuses literature and popular fiction in a way that no other writer has achieved.

In a culture where the creative artist is expected to perform the role of critic, Islwyn Ffowc Elis has used the public platform of eisteddfod adjudication to encourage two generations to read and write intelligently. It is the function of creative prose, he argued in 1965, simply to create:

*Not to record or to describe, not to expound, to air ideas, but to create. To create a new identity, of course, like an essay or a story, but to create at a finer level than that too: to create new metaphors and similes, perhaps new images, word-marriages, which are excitingly new, even though they follow the rules of the language; if recording, to record significantly; if describing, to describe with suggestion; if expounding, to expound as nobody has expounded on the subject before.*

These are counsels of perfection, of course. He admits to being *a bundle of prejudices, like every other man,* reminding an audience unfamiliar with prose fiction that objectivity is meaningless in creative writing. He has been a consistent champion of correct usage, dismissive of claims that great ideas can be expressed in slipshod language.

His greatest achievement, however, has been to articulate a myth, to offer the Welsh a fictional commentary on their common experience. He writes of the diaspora, mixed marriages, the creeping tide of Englishness into rural Wales, the decline of one way of life and the thrilling danger of the new, however prosaic. The novelist's accomplishment, he wrote in 1959, is to fill ordinary events like birth, marriage and death, going to college or falling ill or falling in love, with life and significance. The precise significance of his own contribution can be debated; it cannot, however, be denied.

# II

From the beginning of the twentieth century Eisteddfod Chair and Crown competitions had acted as a finishing school for young poets in a hurry. A winning *awdl* or *pryddest* was a sure-fire way of ensuring a poet an audience for later, more personal work.

The 1930s saw the arrival of a similar means of publicity for prose-writers. The *ysgrif* – best but not perfectly translated as 'essay' – began as the idiosyncratic contribution of one man to the prose renaissance accompanying the standardization of Welsh orthography in 1928. T. H. Parry-Williams's YSGRIFAU, published in the same year, was a donnish, witty and highly stylized series of short pieces on his own reactions to the minutiae of daily life, and his reactions to those reactions. In Welsh that self-consciously veered between the high-flown and the colloquial, T. H. Parry-Williams mused on topics as diverse as an old motor-bike, an egg-timer and the stream of consciousness set in motion during a chapel service on a wet Sunday in Snowdonia. Psychoanalysis met memoir met something that passed for the real world.

For eisteddfod committees in search of prose competitions, the form had the virtues of brevity and an endless supply of subject matter. By early in the following decade competitors were being asked openly to produce volumes *in the style of T. H.*

*Parry-Williams*, literary magazines were filling their pages with the thoughts and fancies of unknown one-work wonders gazing wistfully at teacups and country buses, and the form was rapidly becoming derivative, codified and stale. Islwyn Ffowc Elis's CYN OERI'R GWAED (*Before the Blood Cools*, 1952), while giving the form a transfusion, effectively marked the beginning of the end of the *ysgrif*. The form's most successful innovator and beneficiary was to become, for a while, its most implacable critic.

CYN OERI'R GWAED, Islwyn Ffowc Elis's first major published work, won the Prose Medal at the Llanrwst Eisteddfod in 1951. *I have been in two minds over the years about the value of that little volume*, Islwyn Ffowc Elis wrote in 1973:

*Sometimes I felt that the essays were only juvenile, and often pseudo-poetic, exercises. At others, I would feel – and I feel so now – that I would love to be able to write as well today as I did then. Certainly, I would love to be able to write as easily again.*

There is little in CYN OERI'R GWAED to suggest the path Islwyn Ffowc Elis would take in his more mature work. For one thing, the *ysgrif* cannot but be self-absorbed, the style tight, clipped and epigrammatic, the key minor. Its voice is overwhelmingly conditional or subjunctive. Above all, it is a form necessarily without plot. Firmly in the confessional tradition of T. H. Parry-Williams ('The Master', as Islwyn Ffowc Elis has called him, without irony), CYN OERI'R GWAED is nevertheless unmistakably a young man's work. The opening sentence of the first piece, 'Adfyw' (*Reliving*), *The sun has risen nine thousand times since I first saw it*, has the arithmeticians counting fingers and the title itself conveys something of the desperation of youth as it slides into respectable middle age.

There are certainly fewer weaknesses than strengths. What shortcomings there are emanate, one suspects, from imitation. 'Hyfrydwch y Gwir Grefftwr' (*The Joy of the True Craftsman*) and 'Tai' (*Houses*), for example, are reminiscent of the sort of sententious editorials which O. M. Edwards wrote for his monthly CYMRU at the turn of the century: secular sermons appealing to popular sentiment. In the first we are told that the true craftsman is born, not made; in the second we are asked to consider the social benefits of a rural life-style. We are convinced because we cannot really be bothered to disagree. Others, like 'Gwrychoedd' (*Hedges*) and 'Y Ddannodd' (*Toothache*), are assiduous reworkings of Parry-Williams.

Islwyn Ffowc Elis is at his best when, in accordance with *ysgrif* orthodoxy, he places himself at the centre of the world he has created and indulges in what he has called *the achievement of self-expression*. Often the approach is light. In 'Sut i Yrru Modur' (*How to Drive a Car*), Islwyn Ffowc Elis contends that the ability to drive dehumanizes the driver. Elsewhere, imagination is invoked to enhance the known world by being temporarily free of it. 'Ar Lwybrau Amser' (*On the Paths of Time*) considers time travel. The joy of escape is the tale that one can tell on return. When he writes in 'Mynd i'r Lleuad' (*Going to the Moon*) of *an urge in me, as in every romantic, to escape from where I am and be somewhere else*, he expresses a desire which would become a preoccupation in his major fiction. The real world for him is a place of limitations, an idea conveyed with concision in 'Pe Bawn i'n Wybedyn' (*If I Were a Fly*), where the author ponders the benefits of swapping his consciousness with the instinctual *glorious idiocy* of an insect:

*I too would like to fly on two fine wings. High in the heat, low in a storm. Humming passionately with my peers, without any responsibility towards them, above the warm stench of dunghills. Laying a generation without considering them as family. Eating sewage like dishes fit for a king. Knowing all that a fly needs to know without a day of schooling, without opening a book. Without good or bad, beautiful or repulsive, horizon or ending. And without a dilemma to solve in a cold sweat at the opening of April.*

*And I could have been thus. If Adam hadn't eaten the fruit of the tree and begun to know, tonight I would be nothing more than a glorious fly in a flyless garden. Blessed and with heaven in my eyes, but with no master but my instinct, and desiring nothing more than to be as I am. But Adam ate. And I was born into a world of better and worse, and able to see it as such. And given a task that I cannot complete, hating myself for being what I am and trying to be what I cannot.*

'But Adam Ate' could serve as a subtitle to the volume as a whole. The book is an oxymoron: a study in tongue-in-cheek Calvinism, and Islwyn Ffowc Elis's reflections on the human condition are underpinned almost always by a fall from grace. 'Y Sais' (*The Englishman*), for example, is beyond redemption, *too big to be held in affection, too strong to be pitied, too content with himself to inspire sympathy*. His deliverance will only come with learning *what it is to be second and second-rate*. Humility will teach him gentleness, soften his voice and make him prefer to watch and listen in company rather than seek to dominate:

*On that day he will be loved, and be accepted into the society of the meek, who, somehow or other, inherit the whole earth.*

In the mean time, a common death awaits everyone, to be escaped only through the power of imagination. Imagination can transport a man through time and space and make a mockery of the laws of nature. 'Melodi' (*A Melody*) discusses the phenomenon of a snatch of overheard and unknown music (maybe Rachmaninov or even some hack film-score writer?) and its disproportionate effect on the psyche. He then appears to digress:

*I shall have to die some day. Because I am but a lump of clay which life has borrowed for some years for some purpose about which I can only speculate. And because I met a spirit like this melody in the years of my clayness, death will be more difficult . . . Clay feeling jealous of spirit. One wonders whether the mind of clay which created it and the hands of clay which set it down first on piano keys or violin strings felt the same jealousy. Or did that clay earn immortality for itself by that act of creation?*

In one sense, then, CYN OERI'R GWAED answers its own rhetorical question. It gave its author a handhold on a peculiarly Welsh kind of immortality. Islwyn Ffowc Elis was a recognized writer. In his own phrase, the book helped him to *pocket* the Prose Medal, after which he did not compete in eisteddfodau again.

Islwyn Ffowc Elis has written that CYN OERI'R GWAED owes more in style to the first half of the twentieth century than to the second, comparing the form to the passing charm of lyric poetry. As an adjudicator in the 1954 Eisteddfod, he attacked it as obsolete, coining the word 'ysgrifol' (literally, 'essayish') to dismiss its pattern, sentences and ideas, *most of which are not ideas at all. I am often tempted to think*, he concluded, *that the* ysgrif *is no more than a pleasant way of saying nothing*. It had, however, performed its function as a bridge between poetry and prose. On the strength of this slim and stylish work, Islwyn Ffowc Elis was commissioned to produce his first novel.

By comparison with the delicate prose-style of Cyn Oeri'r Gwaed, Cysgod y Cryman (*The Shadow of the Sickle*, 1953) is epic. It runs to some 80,000 words. Early readers remarked on the pleasantly unfamiliar physical sensation of holding so contemporary and yet so substantial a piece of Welsh fiction in their hands. The story is woven with near-perfect pacing and perceptive, if sometimes rather heavy-handed characterization. It is essentially a tale of conflicting loyalties, the tensions between personal ambition and a sense of continuity, and suffused with a poetic justice.

Even a relatively full summary will leave swathes of the plot untouched. The Vaughans of Lleifior, a thriving farm in the lush Powys countryside of Dyffryn Aerwen, appear to have it all: the patriarchal Edward is rich and well respected, with a shrewd business brain and a seat on the county council. Where he fails to excite admiration, he wins the deference conveyed by the Welsh phrase, 'parchedig ofn'. His wife, Margaret (like so many other wives in Islwyn Ffowc Elis's work), is the perfect partner, his daughter, Greta, is dutiful and pretty, an embodiment of 'blonde nimbleness'. Moreover, the eldest child, Harri, has added a Bangor BA and a local fiancée of good stock,

Lisabeth, to the family's store. Lleifior is crammed with tradition. The family's arms are emblazoned over the mantelpiece. Harri is heir apparent to a comfortable existence: *nothing remained for Harri except to become a gentleman for the rest of his life.*

Deftly, the props which support Harri's place in the world are removed. The story opens with Harri's return to Lleifior at the end of his finals. His summer holidays helping with the harvest become an opportunity to introduce the other protagonists: most notably, the saintly Karl Weissman, a German ex-prisoner of war with impeccable Welsh. Karl is a six-foot Aryan monument to erudition, faith in God, and noble suffering; he has even been taught to lose at chess with dignity. Karl's wartime experiences have left him with a fatalistic view of civilization: *'The genius of the West is exhausted'*, he tells Harri. *'Tired'*. Since civilization cannot go forward, it must look back.

A departure from the expected route is inevitable. The first victim of Harri's moral revisionism is Lisabeth, the seemingly perfect match for a wealthy young man in need of a wife. She is a vision in a white angora cardigan, beautiful, faithful and a little dull. Against a backdrop *which could have been painted by Turner*, the storm clouds gather.

On the field of the National Eisteddfod, Harri is bewitched by the feisty Gwylan, a Communist whose articles on the inevitable march of the 'socialist vision' and dark eyes will eventually convince him to reject both Lisabeth and his inheritance. He spends the rest of the summer in a quandary.

Autumn comes. Harri returns to Bangor as a postgraduate and finds himself greeted by Gwylan as *on the point of conversion* to world-wide revolution. While Harri ponders the ethics of opposing Franco, the fate of blacks in South Africa and the moral bankruptcy of inherited wealth, back at Lleifior Margaret Vaughan falls ill. She is saved by the intervention of Paul Rushmere, a brilliant young doctor from Liverpool, whose pursuit of Greta is encouraged by her parents. Although uncertain herself, she marries him, disappointing the besotted Karl and leaving the door open for a sequel where justice can be done.

Harri returns to Dyffryn Aerwen for the Christmas holidays with a set of Lenin's complete writings in his luggage:

*It was as if he were coming to an unfamiliar place, where everyone belonged to a different world and age and mentality to his own. From his perspective, the previous term had turned everyone and everything upside down. Gwylan had happened.*

He has no time to read them. Persuaded by Gwylan that all private farms will be *going through the mincer in the next twenty years*, Harri breaks his engagement with Lisabeth. The ailing Margaret finds the truth in a letter from Lisabeth's mother among the Christmas cards. Worse is to follow: Edward discovers one of the offending books on Harri's bedside table. Harri is forced to choose between his £25,000 inheritance and his principles. He chooses the latter.

This act of self-determination prompts a crisis. For Harri, student life at Bangor suddenly appears *superficial and childish . . . as if he were looking over park railings at children playing.* He determines on leaving academia for the simpler, more noble life of a common labourer. At Lleifior, Margaret's condition becomes critical and she is rushed to hospital. Lisabeth's father, Robert Pugh, meanwhile, plots Edward's defeat in the forthcoming election. Greta and Karl fall deeply but unwittingly in love.

Harri spends the night of his mother's treatment in Liverpool at the Socialist Society dinner, torn between filial concern and a feeling for Gwylan which is something strangely akin to

*admiring her as a man would admire his political hero or a schoolgirl a film star. Over the previous months, it was she who had nursed and matured him into the powerful mentality of the common people which he now possessed. She had been a scourge and a balm, a storm and a rock. Harri began to smile as he heard his thoughts expressing themselves so poetically. But the smile faded. They were true. She had been all these things to him. And more.*

Poised to reveal the extent of this admiration for her by announcing his decision to leave Bangor behind, Harri learns that his own enthusiasm for the cause has made Gwylan question the depth of her own commitment. She falls apart, publicly renouncing Communism, inviting Harri to marry her and indulging in an unseemly display of passion, pulling him onto her *locking her arms and legs around him like an octopus attacking a fish.* The spell is broken. He walks away, leaving her a dishevelled, whining wreck,

*unable to stand the difference between the sharp, super-ethical heroine she had been for whom he would have sacrificed his life* three hours before, and the inhuman thing twitching before him in the undergrowth behind the bench.

Having won the moral battle with Gwylan, Harri returns to Lleifior, is reconciled with his father, marries the capable Marged from the village council estate and takes over running the farm as a co-operative. The novel ends with a sunset falling on the Vaughan crest.

The composition of CYSGOD Y CRYMAN, Islwyn Ffowc Elis has commented, *flowed so appallingly easily* that he felt a duty to learn the craft of novel-writing properly, *so that I would be sure what a novel was and how it should be written professionally*. Interestingly, he has compared his experience with that of the eighteenth-century hymn-writer Williams Pantycelyn in composing the epic poem, BYWYD A MARWOLAETH THEOMEMPHUS (*The Life and Death of Theomemphus*, 1764): *This book rolled out from my soul like . . . a spider's web from its own belly*.

It is illuminating to extend the comparison to the content of the two works. Pantycelyn's eponymous hero can be seen, very broadly, as a juvenile counterpart of Bunyan's Pilgrim, a Candide with a soul or the embodiment of the parable of the Prodigal Son. The poem follows the spiritual journey of the young man to redemption. He is tempted by conflicting sophistries, is offered false hopes, strays wilfully and in the end learns that salvation depends on an acknowledgement of sin and submission to grace. Although Islwyn Ffowc Elis would reserve offering an overtly religious dimension to Harri's character until CYSGOD Y CRYMAN's sequel, YN ÔL I LLEIFIOR (*Return to Lleifior*) three years later, the framework of

Cysgod y Cryman certainly owes something to a similar dynamic of conversion.

Where the comparison with Theomemphus and the rest breaks down spectacularly, of course, is that Cysgod y Cryman stands unmistakeably within the realist tradition. Harri and the rest of Islwyn Ffowc Elis's creations live in a recognizable society. Islwyn Ffowc Elis's achievement is to place the parable of the Prodigal Son in the specific context of post-war Wales. With Cysgod y Cryman he opened the Welsh novel to a range of situations hitherto unexplored. It is a commentary on the opportunities and dangers of social mobility. Lleifior finds it difficult to recruit farm-hands, Liberalism is in seemingly terminal decline, Communism is a force in intellectual circles and a crude kind of egalitarianism – embodied in the feckless Wil James – challenges the natural order. Moreover, there are the inferences which Welsh-speaking readers would instinctively take from the text. In the early 1950s Greta's marriage to Paul Rushmere would almost certainly mean that any offspring would be English-speaking, perhaps the most compelling reason in most readers' minds why the two should not marry. Gwylan, as a native of industrial Dyffryn Nantlle, represents a Welshness which explains both her politics and her character. Harri's room-mate at university, Gwdig, exhibits the fresh-faced earnestness and almost evangelical fervour of nationalism in an age of electoral disappointment. There is even a wily piece of dialogue in 'Bangor Welsh' from a railway porter.

The novel creaks when the authorial voice tells the reader what the reader can be reasonably expected to discover without help. More often than not, these centre on observations of character: *They were both men*, Islwyn Ffowc Elis says of Harri and his father on Harri's return home at the beginning of the novel, for example, *flesh of the same flesh, flesh which became shy touching itself.* Or,

*Gentleness got under Wil James's skin. His world was a world of hard voices and bitter replies, and nobody had any business answering him politely.*

At other times, the author speaks in generalities in a way which calls to mind the apprentice *ysgrifwr* of CYN OERI'R GWAED. Harri receiving news of his mother's illness, for instance, is prefaced by a paragraph which could have appeared at any one of a dozen points in the book:

*The bitter things in life come unannounced. Like thieves in the night when men are dancing. To disturb joy and explode the delicious monotony of living.*

It is customary for commentators to discuss Islwyn Ffowc Elis's second novel, FFENESTRI TUA'R GWYLL (*Windows Towards the Dusk*, 1955), in parentheses, regarding it as a free-standing, almost aberrant creation which interrupted the narrative integrity of CYSGOD Y CRYMAN and YN ÔL I LEIFIOR, where the stories of Harri, Greta, Karl and the rest are continued and concluded. A strictly chronological approach is, however, an interesting exercise in tracing the technical lessons which Islwyn Ffowc Elis felt he needed to learn. FFENESTRI TUA'R GWYLL shunned sage remarks in favour of introspection. Its central character, the forty-something widow Ceridwen Morgan, a provincial Lady Ottoline Morrell or Lady Gregory, holds court at the palatial

Trem-y-Gorwel overlooking the seaside town of Caerwenlli. Frustrated despite (or more precisely because of) her wealth and leisure, the childless Ceridwen suppresses the memory of an unhappy marriage, glorying vicariously in her role as muse and confidante, *a means for others to make a name, an opportunity for others to shine.* She supports, houses and pays the drinking bills of the witty but graceless homosexual Cecil, a 'modern' artist of questionable talent; has the lovelorn novelist Idris Jenkins dedicate his racy *Youth Was My Sin* to her; tolerates the erudite, tedious 'holy snake', Reverend Sirian Owen; and thrives on the attention of Bob Pritchard, whose collection of mature verse, *Aeron yr Hydref*, seems set to mark him out as Wales's greatest living poet. Looks, bearing, acuity, grace and a deep, cool well of self-worth just about keep Ceridwen Morgan from the neuroses of snobbery and despair which afflict those around her. Her life is measured out in intimate suppers *à deux* and shared confidences, like a secular mother-confessor. The tensions within her salon, Cecil's fecklessness, Idris's passion, Bob's bluff conservatism and Sirian's wilful occupation of the moral high ground can never be reconciled, but can be borne.

Downfall comes with that most Welsh of all crises: a damning poetry review in a literary magazine. Alfan Ellis, a gauche young poet praised (and lusted after) by Cecil, becomes a house guest at Trem-y-Gorwel. As a Welsh learner from the Rhondda, an outsider untutored in the niceties of such things, Alfan has no qualms about dismissing the lyrical charm of *Aeron yr Hydref* as *childish play with experiences . . . versifying clink-clonk*. Bob Pritchard, who in his ignorance had allowed himself the indulgence of wanting just one bad notice to leaven the dough of praise, is shattered. Despite Ceridwen's protestations, Alfan repeats the offence on radio. A celebration of Bob Pritchard's life and work hosted by Ceridwen at the house degenerates into farce. The centre cannot hold.

The ending teeters on the edge of the gothic. Ceridwen, like her namesake in the legend of Taliesin, tries to adopt Alfan as son-cum-lover. She sets aside the best room for him at Trem-y-Gorwel and throws out Cecil. The sweet, simple Nesta, Alfan's fiancée, is invited, inspected, humiliated and dismissed. Ceridwen sees in Alfan a means of escape from the ghost of her dead husband, Ceredig, whose grinning portrait hangs over the mantelpiece, from the social claustrophobia and wreckage of Caerwenlli, and from her own impending old age. Caught, in Sirian's words,

*in the gap between the wholeness of youth and the second wholeness of old age . . . that gap of disillusionment, where dreams are shreds and intentions broken shards . . .*

she makes a last, desperate act of creation, moulding Alfan in the image of a more perfect Ceredig. Alfan, dressed in Ceredig's own clothes, is asked to re-enact a violent rape to exorcize his memory. The venture ends, inevitably, in insanity. Alfan is reconciled with Nesta and Ceridwen is seen for the last time as a befuddled, harmless and prematurely senile woman.

With FFENESTRI TUA'R GWYLL, Islwyn Ffowc Elis moves from the overt moral criticism and approbation of CYSGOD Y CRYMAN to a more ambiguous position. The development is as much one of literary technique as ethics. By creating a strong, complex central figure in

Ceridwen, Islwyn Ffowc Elis allows characters to shift, compromise, play off one another and earn our commendation or reproach by virtue of their own actions with regard to her. Everything is filtered through the mesh of Ceridwen's own prejudices and preconceptions, and because her own moral standing ultimately proves to be as precarious as any other character's, the narrative is sustained more by our ambivalence than by any sympathy or censure demanded of us. Her moral world enhances the characters who live within it, and Islwyn Ffowc Elis's deliberately hands-off technique reveals shades and depths even in the most bizarre creations, like Cecil. Where a character fails to be more than a cypher – as with the odious Catrin Prys-Roberts – it is because, although they serve the plot, their significance to Ceridwen is minimal. Most important, the intrusive and occasionally arch authorial voice of CYSGOD Y CRYMAN is mute. It is a novel of showing, not telling. What telling there is, is carefully mediated through the interior voices of the characters. For example, when Ceridwen closes Bob Pritchard's book of verse, it is her voice we hear and the irony is implicit in the refocusing thoughts of the silent character who makes them:

*Ceridwen closed* Aeron yr Hydref *and placed it lovingly on her lap. There was no doubt about Bob Pritchard's greatness. Fifteen years was not too long to wait for this volume; it was worth waiting another fifteen years for it. Every poem instantly became a thrill in the blood – apart from two or three perhaps, and there was a weak poem in every book of poetry ever published . . .*

*To fill her cup to overflowing, Bob had, after all, dedicated the volume to her. Not by name, unfortunately . . . But it was obvious that the book had been dedicated to a female, and the book-worms of the future would be eager to know which female.*

*Their search for her name would not be as hopeless as their search for the name of Shakespeare's Dark Lady. And it was quite possible that her immortality would be more certain because of the debate surrounding her.*

Despite its superior technical accomplishment, FFENESTRI TUA'R GWYLL has, not surprisingly, been a less popular work than CYSGOD Y CRYMAN. Islwyn Ffowc Elis has described it as *an experiment – the rather desperate one of a young and ambitious novelist to write a work for the critics.* It lacks the qualities that make his first novel such a good read. There are no cinematic sweeps of landscape and observations of nature as backdrop, very little scene-switching, black humour has replaced comedy, and, because of the novel's reliance on Ceridwen, the few scenes where she does not appear tend to be flat. A novel of interiors, the narrative relies heavily on conversation and the pace is ponderous. In a sense FFENESTRI TUA'R GWYLL marks the obverse of the shining New Elizabethanism of CYSGOD Y CRYMAN, depicting a 'tired age', as Islwyn Ffowc Elis's literary hero Tegla Davies once said.

Welcoming the reprint of FFENESTRI TUA'R GWYLL in 1997, Gerwyn Williams noted that the Welsh novel of the 1960s and 1970s owed more in style, matter and sensibility to Islwyn Ffowc Elis's self-acknowledged failure than to the hugely more successful CYSGOD Y CRYMAN. The point is well made: one can certainly picture Ceridwen and the rest at home in the pages of a Jane Edwards or R. Gerallt Jones novel. Indeed, it could be argued the foundations of Islwyn Ffowc Elis's own subsequent popular acclaim were laid in this second period of apprenticeship. FFENESTRI TUA'R GWYLL taught its author the value of allowing the interior lives of characters to express themselves in trivial actions. In Cysgod y Cryman, characters say what they mean and mean what they say; here, on the other hand, their behaviour betrays their true motives. Ceridwen sits in her own picture window, not only to enjoy (or criticize) the view but also to be an object of admiration and curiosity herself. She plays the *Sonata Pathétique* first to herself and then to Alfan as an act of seduction through good taste.

Ffenestri tua'r Gwyll taught Islwyn Ffowc Elis the power of irony. Read through its lens, the saintly Karl of Yn Ôl i Leifior can be legitimately criticized as a prig; Huw Prydderch in Blas y Cynfyd becomes less of an innocent abroad, and the bumbling Ifans in Tabyrddau'r Babongo emerges more sympathetic than pathetic. It also introduced a related dimension into Islwyn Ffowc Elis's prose, described by him in a 1962 lecture on Thema yn y Nofel Gymraeg (*Theme in the Welsh Novel*) as the preserve of any mature novel:

> *Hypocrisy is a slow-working poison, and a man sees it in other people before seeing it in himself. That is why a novelist cannot write well about hypocrisy until he is middle-aged, has learned to be one person at work, another person to his friends, yet another person to his children, and has been confounded and disappointed by the hypocrisy of others.*

Ceridwen's hypocrisy is only realized by the reader when her fate is assured; we want to find her laughable, but her own self-belief is such that she carries the reader with her further than is comfortable. Perhaps the 'failure' of Ffenestri tua'r Gwyll lies here: in being written ahead of its time by a talent without the compensatory weight of experience. It has been said that it would be enough of a challenge for a middle-aged woman to write convincingly of a woman's mid-life crisis, let alone a man in his early thirties. The technical legacy to Islwyn Ffowc Elis as a writer, though, was incalculable. The perennial problem of writing a second novel had been surmounted, and whereas CYSGOD Y CRYMAN had by its author's own admission been inspired, FFENESTRI TUA'R GWYLL was the product of sustained hard work.

Another indication of the achievement of FFENESTRI TUA'R GWYLL lies in a comparison with Islwyn Ffowc Elis's long-forgotten scrap of a short story, 'Merch Caligwla' (a misprint for MARCH CALIGWLA, *Caligula's Horse*), published in YR EFRYDYDD in 1950. Subtitled *An Academic Tale*, it anticipates the Caerwenlli community in a crude piece of satire on the inhabitants of an aesthetic group. Andro Lewis writes obscure verse; the minister Euryn Brown thrives on criticism, *for him it was like rain for a duck, or, perhaps, a spur to a rocking horse*; Morys murders the piano in homage to a neglected German composer. Theoretical Communists all, worshippers at the shrine of the 'Indestructible Proletariat', they call out a plumber on the pretext of having burst pipes. Their unofficial leader, Elveta (a sketchy prototype of CYSGOD Y CRYMAN's Gwylan Thomas), admits the deception to him:

'*Do you see. We are here to worship the Common Man. He is our king. And we wanted you to come here with your tools and in your work clothes, to sweep us off our feet. Here are the members of the Cult. And now they wish to rise to their feet as a sign of their devotion – to you.*'

*And the company rose obediently, staring transfixedly at the Being. Second after second passed through the room. Then, without turning a hair, the Being took a step towards the fire and spat into it liberally, and having thrown his sackful of tools over his shoulder, he walked out of the room and through the lobby into the night, slamming the door behind him.*

*The Cult stood there eyeing one another across the furniture, and there was nothing to be heard but the sound of the Being's spit frying in the fire.*

The story closes there, with the chatter of the poet and minister and artist and the rest silenced by an epiphany which might be disgust, disenchantment or the fulfilment of their hopes. It hardly matters; the target of the satire, at the end of the story as at the beginning, is political and artistic pretension. Elveta, Andro and Euryn and the rest do not develop; the opinion the author insists we have of them has already been wrung out of us in the opening half-dozen paragraphs. The outcome of the story merely serves to make the reader feel justified in espousing a view which is satisfyingly confirmed in the gratuitous act of a nameless, no-nonsense plumber. The interest of MARCH CALIGWLA is as a prototype of what FFENESTRI TUA'R GWYLL might have been had it lacked irony and technical control of voice.

Between them, CYSGOD Y CRYMAN and FFENESTRI TUA'R GWYLL neatly convey the distinction popularly drawn in criticism of the 1950s and 1960s between *contemporary* and *modern* fiction. CYSGOD Y CRYMAN's voice is contemporary: politically aware, propagandist and imbued with an optimism that the circumstances in which the characters find themselves are capable of amelioration. FFENESTRI TUA'R GWYLL, in contrast, is modern. Its style is more rarefied, its sensibility more disaffected, its characters inclined to detest their circumstances to a degree where hopelessness becomes the dominant emotion. There is a fatalism about modern fiction which the contemporary novelist would view as self-indulgence; an underlying optimism in the contemporary which the modern would regard as trivial.

The distinction is best illustrated by the way in which the lives of the novels' chief protagonists are depicted. CYSGOD Y CRYMAN is slice-of-life fiction: what the medieval Welsh might have called Harri Vaughan's *mabinogi* or youthful exploits. Harri graduates, falls in and out of love, espouses politics, argues with his father, is reconciled, and eventually reaches an accommodation with which he, those around him and the reader all feel comfortable. The progress of Ceridwen Morgan's life, on the other hand, is sketchy and its events largely incidental. Her tragedy pivots on a relationship which is never fully explained and her window high above Caerwenlli becomes a metaphor for the cynical detachment which the reader is eventually obliged to share.

Curiously, CYSGOD Y CRYMAN was a more experimental, certainly a braver, piece of fiction than FFENESTRI TUA'R GWYLL. With the ebullient exception of Daniel Owen at the very end of the nineteenth century, the novel in Welsh had contained very little with a contemporary feel. Conscious, no doubt, of the difficulty of depicting society with a broad brush in a language which was geographically and socially limited, Welsh novelists had tended towards the smaller canvas of introspection. Kate Roberts's TRAED MEWN CYFFION (*Feet in Chains*, 1936), for example, widely accepted as the first genuine novel of the twentieth century, is essentially a critique of contemporary Wales dressed as an epic, where the trials of a family over the period roughly between 1890 and 1918 are meant to be seen through the lens of a later, less ingenuous age. The same could be said of T. Rowland Hughes's CHWALFA (*Dispersal*, 1946) with its corresponding story of past social upheaval. Published only seven years later, CYSGOD Y CRYMAN belongs to a different era, ready to embrace the present for all its faults.

Even the title of the delayed sequel to CYSGOD Y CRYMAN, YN ÔL I LEIFIOR, can be interpreted as a retreat from the claustrophobia of FFENESTRI TUA'R GWYLL to the surer ground of family relationships. It marked, of course, Islwyn Ffowc Elis's first conscious attempt to write with one eye on sales figures, and its serialization on radio prior to publication was a boon. Peopled by a cast of familiar, sympathetic characters and rounded by a redemptive ending, the book has both a domesticity and a spiritual depth anticipated in CYSGOD Y CRYMAN but only capable of realization here.

It is a tale of beginnings and endings. The novel opens with the burial of Margaret Vaughan, Harri's mother, marking the end of a generation and drawing attention to Harri's continuing disaffection with religion. He attends the funeral unable to believe in an afterlife and incapable of making sense of a divine plan which separates a loving couple like his parents yet allows Greta and Paul to be thrown together in a pointless marriage. *Such a thing wasn't a plan, but the devilment of fate. Everything on earth was an accident.* Harri's spiritual quest becomes an implicit critique of the genre itself. The author of CYSGOD Y CRYMAN, who had implied that a novel revolves around unpredictable reverses of fortune, now ties loose ends together, simultaneously making sense of divine providence and providing the reader with a gratifying conclusion. In YN ÔL I LEIFIOR, Christian apologetics serves popular fiction and vice versa in roughly equal measure.

The novel draws both its plot and its moral dynamic from the humbling of Harri and his sister Greta's corresponding self-discovery. Harri, as he did in CYSGOD Y CRYMAN, begins the novel as hero. He has now developed Lleifior as a successful co-operative farm, made the business into a model of enlightened, disciplined democracy, has *a wife from the proletariat* (Harri's own words) and a bright button of a son, colleagues whom he trusts and the respect of his father. In a telling metaphor, Edward Vaughan surrenders the farm to a new generation. Taking advantage of his children's absence from Lleifior one evening, he looks with awe and incomprehension at the changes brought about on the farm he once controlled. Suddenly he is disturbed:

*He heard the sound of a car turning from the road and coming up the drive to the house. He turned at the door, and stared straight into the young, defiant light aimed towards him. He knew that his children were behind the light, seeing in the light that blinded him. He felt the light judging him as he stood there, showing him clearly as he was, an elderly man who was beginning to stoop and for whose tired brain life was too much of a puzzle. He hoped that his children who saw him there would judge him mercifully, and would be ready to forgive him for being so blind where they, perhaps, could see.*

As Edward Vaughan slips into a fond and foolish dotage, reconciled to his own mortality, closer to God than he had been for years, Harri kicks over the traces. He pronounces himself open-minded on matters of belief. His wife's assumption that their son Huw Powys should be baptized provokes a tirade:

*I don't believe in God. I'm not saying that there isn't Something greater than man in creation, some . . . Spirit, if you like, which is the start and centre of everything. But I'll never get to find out more about him, and I can't know him. He's nothing to do with me, and I'm nothing to do with Him. The God I heard too much about when I was a child – Our Father Who art in Heaven, and so on – He doesn't exist for me. I think that He is the creation of one class of people's imagination, no more than an extension of their own minds, something to depend upon after they have grown too old to depend on parents.*

The words are loaded with irony, of course, ready to explode spectacularly in Harri's face. Equally interesting is to consider how well the author succeeds in accommodating abstract chunks like these within the structure of a popular novel whose professed function is to show rather than tell. Out of context, this set piece reads like third-rate Mauriac. It is a measure of Islwyn Ffowc Elis's ability that not only do Harri's words arise naturally out of the story so far, but that they advance the plot and illuminate his and Marged's character at the same time. Harri's speech is polished and cogent because it is the stuff of a hundred late-night college conversations. Even the shape of their exchanges on the page – Harri's slabs of text interspersed with Marged's one-line responses – are an indication of his dependence on language and her quiet persistence. The clash between Harri's theorizing and Marged's conventionality ('*I think that the baptism of a baby is the prettiest thing there is,*' she counters at one point) establishes a tension in the relationship that will be tried again before the novel's close. The fissure of guilt in Harri's character, through which he will glimpse the light of redemption, is almost imperceptibly opened.

The conversation also highlights the point already made earlier about the mutual dependence of theology and popular fiction in Yn Ôl i Leifior. Before Harri can be saved, he must learn to believe without understanding. His conversion must be as much an aesthetic as a religious education, a willing suspension of disbelief, a leap of faith which implies a corresponding leap of the imagination. When Harri claims that there is no *sense* (his italics) in baptism, Marged's retort is significant: '*Is there sense in dew on a rose?*' Harri is floored. As an instinctive reductionist, baptism is no more than two droplets of water on a child's head. His natural modes of thought are the theoretical and the practical application of theory.

Up until the deaths of his father and son his life is a flight from exercising his imagination. At a cinema in London, Harri is taken with the travelogue on Canada, but can't even coax his critical faculties to stay awake during the main feature. Left alone with a book of Damon Runyon stories on his sick-bed and a command to relax, Harri surreptitiously takes up his postgraduate thesis on Marxism in rural Wales. His transition from ethical atheist to penitent Christian needs the twin fillip of the unimaginable and the intellectually respectable. This is manifested in the death of Huw Powys at Lleifior just as Harri almost succumbs to the charms of Vera in London, and a model of faith in the new minister.

Gareth Evans MA, a contemporary of Harri, is the *honnête homme* of liberal Nonconformism. The shelves of his library contain Welsh religious periodicals, Chaucer, Sheridan, Dickens, D. H. Lawrence, Welsh literature and Plaid Cymru pamphlets. In him Harri finds an intellectual equal; Gareth meanwhile looks to Harri as a confessor.

Their mutual dependence is the pivot on which this part of the book turns. Gareth confides his own feelings of inadequacy as a minister to Harri and in turn becomes Harri's spiritual mentor, assuring him that his peccadillo in London has broken down the 'moral smugness' which has kept him from salvation. *You had to commit some sin which you yourself couldn't forgive*, he tells the self-loathing Harri, *to make you conscious of Sin – with a capital S. You were a good boy before. But your damnation lay in your goodness.* A chastened Harri undergoes his transformation and Gareth feels that his role is justified.

While Harri agonizes, his sister Greta undergoes her own crises of faith. Trapped in Liverpool, she challenges her husband's High Church Toryism and asserts her selfhood by joining the local branch of Plaid Cymru:

*The great rush and peevishness and uneasiness had stopped dead, and Greta was standing in her existential moment, knowing for the first time ever what she was. She was nothing in that naked moment, but Greta: Greta Lleifior standing on a foreign pavement, refusing everything around her, and discovering herself, what she was, a piece of Wales.*

It offers a temporary respite, but ultimately sets in train the events which lead to Paul's death as he races to Wales to save the marriage, prompting the guilt which threatens to submerge Greta. The bipolar structure of the novel – the interleaving of Greta and Harri's contrasting dilemmas – makes explicit a key aspect of the characterization in Islwyn Ffowc Elis's early fiction: while his men act on principle, his women are motivated by a sense of obligation. Harri's flaw is an absence of guilt, Greta suffers a surfeit. Her self-denial becomes a sickness. Like some fairy-tale princess who cannot smile, she turns away prospective suitors while she dwells on her own loss, caught *in the abyss between the desire to die and the desire to live.*

In the same way that Gareth Evans acts as a catalyst for Harri's reprieve, Greta has her own misery demystified for her by Dr Maldwyn Edwards. Her nationalism, he tells her, is incidental to her wider failure to live with Paul, a symptom of their unhappiness, not a cause. That same conviction can be a force for good, a reason to live.

*Put flesh and blood on your conviction. Work. Sweat . . . You have a cause to fight for, and your health lies in that cause, never mind the health of Wales.*

Delyth George has rightly remarked that Greta's nationalism is a narrative blind alley. Her activity is confined to selling literature at a local show and attending a conference. What tenderness there is in her is lavished on Huw Powys. His redemptive death prompts both his father's spiritual deliverance and his aunt's decision to embrace life. In comforting the grieving parents, she learns to reconcile herself to losing Paul. The vacuum left in her own emotions is conveniently filled by Karl's return from exile in England to join the co-operative. The book concludes with the kiss between Greta and Karl which the author had tantalizingly withheld since the middle of CYSGOD Y CRYMAN. The sleeping princess awakes.

The Lleifior novels between them have the moral and narrative completeness of a Shakespeare comedy in which wrongs are righted and a discernible justice prevails. The working out of Harri and Greta's dilemmas gave Islwyn Ffowc Elis a set of controlling principles which were to become the staple of his longer fiction: true happiness is hard-won; frailties can only be healed by being acknowledged; reconciliation lies in compromise; there is a place for everyone and everything, however reluctant some people are to recognize it. His fiction thereafter would be the application of these to a changing Wales and beyond. Although Islwyn Ffowc Elis introduced a new generation to the Vaughans and their circle in a popular eight-part television series in early 1993, LLEIFIOR served merely as a convenient setting for a drama which had already been played out some forty years before.

# III

Islwyn Ffowc Elis's first spell as a full-time writer produced a range of fiction in which it was already possible to hear a consistent narrative voice and discern a moral direction. His next novel, however, might be most charitably described as a distraction. WYTHNOS YNG NGHYMRU FYDD (*A Week in the New Wales*, 1957) was published originally by Plaid Cymru. Islwyn Ffowc Elis has described it in a favourite epithet as 'unashamedly' political. The book purports to be the diary of Ifan Powel, a socialist, whose two journeys through time from 1953 to the Wales of 2033 transform him into a committed nationalist.

The first Wales Ifan visits is a utopia built in the image of Plaid's Ten Policy Points of 1933. She is free, Christian, democratic and completely bilingual. A benevolent administration ensures full employment in co-operative units, rural depopulation has been reversed and Wales is an active member of a federation of pacifist European statelets. Old-world values – the quarrymen in Bethesda touch their caps to ladies – exist alongside an enlightened wider world where the H-bomb has been eradicated. British unionism has been reduced to a paramilitary rump. Progressive taxation restricts the growth of monopolies and strikes are almost unheard of. Thanks to a benevolent penal system, Wales enjoys the lowest crime rates in Europe, the charm offensive of ecumenism has defeated denominationalism and child-centred education has produced a generation of well-adjusted citizens confident in their Welshness and familiar with the wider world. Fashionable French, Spanish and Germans listen avidly to *cerdd dant*, traditional singing to the counter-melody of a harp; vineyards and banana plantations thrive in the Teifi valley thanks to imported sunshine, and the miners of Nantgarw enjoy three months a year in the open air. A statue of Saunders Lewis stands in Cardiff city centre and even the football at Ninian Park is worth watching:

*It was a rich country, and in an age which had accomplished the unbelievable but had still kept its head. The old rush and drunkenness of the twentieth century had gone. These Welsh could embrace progress with circumspection and achievement with humility.*

Ifan is persuaded by Doctor Heinkel, the German scientist who has made the trip possible, to return to the present, but love for the raven-haired beauty Mair Llywarch draws him back to the future. The second Wales he finds has been renamed Western England, a nightmare of urban decay, mob rule and bureaucracy. In the company of an eccentric professor who has learned Welsh, Ifan sets off on a journey to discover whether anything remains of the Wales he once knew. Half the country is under afforestation, Aberystwyth is a maze of *steel-and-concrete flats, pubs, chip shops, saloons, dance halls and gambling dens*, the National Library has become a hotel and the villages of the west are so many numbered ruins, their names unpronounceable to the people who live there. Mair is now Maria Clark and works in a chemist's. Ifan weeps:

*I was weeping, not out of anger at the vandals who had done all this – it was obvious that they knew not what they did – but out of anger at my own generation, the generation to whose care all these treasures had been entrusted, who had allowed the swine to rush in and ruin them. I was sure that heaven would never forgive the Welsh, or me, for selling our heritage so cheap, so blasphemously, appallingly cheap.*

In virtually the final scene, Ifan meets a befuddled old lady in the stinking back room of a shop in Bala. She sometimes mutters to herself in an incomprehensible language, her daughter tells him. The language proves, of course, to be Welsh. Ifan takes her hand and together they recite the closing words of the Twenty-third Psalm. The old woman becomes animated, then rambles and falls silent. The scene concludes with the one line in Islwyn Ffowc Elis's canon which anyone who has read the book cannot fail to remember: *I had seen with my own eyes the death of the Welsh language*. It is a hugely affecting piece; a victory of artist over propagandist which almost, *almost* redeems the whole. If Islwyn Ffowc Elis had left Ifan there, perhaps it would have. Unfortunately, the book lingers long enough to save Ifan from his fate and return him to the Wales of 1953, a wiser man.

What Dickens tried to achieve for the secular Victorian Christmas by showing Scrooge his own gravestone in A CHRISTMAS CAROL, Islwyn Ffowc Elis tried to do for Welsh nationalism here. WYTHNOS YNG NGHYMRU FYDD was an inappropriate vehicle for the task. *I did not intend it to be a novel*, he said of it twenty-five years later. He has spoken of it elsewhere as *a story not fit to be treated as literature*. It is nevertheless a worthwhile critical exercise to see how exactly the work fails. The most common criticism of WYTHNOS YNG NGHYMRU FYDD is that the utopian section, which accounts for a good three-quarters of the novel, is so worthy and dull. Who would really want to live there? One is reminded of William Morris's NEWS FROM NOWHERE, where the citizens all greet the visitor with a ready-made speech and an appreciative awareness of their situation. The second, darker Wales is more arresting (and probably closer to the Wales which Islwyn Ffowc Elis's readers knew in 1957), but the after-image of the utopia inevitably distorts the dystopia. The narrative becomes a check-list of contrasts. It fails as a novel because it lacks the weight and warmth of a novel. The story demands a sustained narrative because of the sheer amount of information the author feels obliged to include to support his future visions, but the framework is too flimsy. When one compares WYTHNOS YNG NGHYMRU FYDD with Islwyn Ffowc Elis's successful fiction, it is clear that it also founders because of its simplistic, formulaic plotting. The expansive Islwyn Ffowc Elis of the Lleifior novels is hampered by a narrative of correspondences, a structure which demands Ifan's presence throughout, and a story where simultaneity, the staple of his best fiction, is necessarily absent. The work is further undermined by its all-Wales scope; the intimate and the private are surrendered.

Moreover, the circumstances of its composition and its central character make it all but impossible for the work to succeed. Written at the request of and presented to Plaid Cymru, it stands in the tradition of the type of testimonial propaganda which was the party's preferred means of publicity at the time. One feels that the spirit of WYTHNOS YNG NGHYMRU FYDD could easily be accommodated *mutatis mutandis* within the contemporary series of essays, PAHAM YR WYF YN AELOD O BLAID CYMRU (*Why I am a Member of Plaid Cymru*) in which the party converts spoke earnestly about the experiences which led them to espouse the cause. Propaganda of the sort succeeds or fails, of course, to the extent that the reader identifies or fails to identify with the narrator. Despite the author's attempt to make Ifan as ordinary as possible, the character straddles two moral dimensions. He is at the same time unique and ordinary, anodyne and exceptional, an Everyman in extraordinary circumstances. Nor does the simplistic plot equip him to be the accidental hero which might have redeemed him.

Criticism has concentrated as much on genre as on content, as if critics felt squeamish with a crude propaganda label. R. M. Jones has called it 'a children's book?' (his question mark); John Rowlands has hinted that it contains elements of medieval romance, particularly in its descriptions of Mair Llywarch. W. J. Jones has given it a cautious welcome as *the first space novel in the Welsh language*, evidence of the author's desire to draw his readers away from the domesticity of the Lleifior novels, arguing that

*if the political consciousness behind [it] had not been so strong it is certain that it could have developed into a truly interesting novel.*

Perhaps a compromise would be to call it a science fable, the application of the model of H. G. Wells's 'scientific romance' to the particular circumstances of mid-twentieth-century Wales. An interest in time travel certainly pre-dates Islwyn Ffowc Elis's earliest published fiction. In the CYN OERI'R GWAED *ysgrif*, 'Ar Lwybrau Amser', already referred to, he expresses a curiosity about using a Wells-style machine to travel forward *to see how Wales will be when the next page turns*:

> A thoroughly Welsh-speaking Wales or an English-speaking or Russian-speaking Wales; a free Wales or a Wales which won't be Wales.

Faced with the opportunity to pursue the idea, Islwyn Ffowc Elis chose to introduce a political imperative. Which Wales will the reader choose? In so doing he created a strange amalgam of nineteenth-century utopianism and twentieth-century despair, making Wales past and Wales future subservient to a third and more urgent Wales of the present. The two versions of Wales he creates require an observer and a first-person narrative, but the demands the author places on Ifan in each section vary. In the first, idealized Wales he is passive, a conduit, a means for the socio-political system to be explained and explored. By the second part, he becomes a dissident, required to act against the system. The devil has all the best tunes, of course: the Dark Wales is pacier, more vibrant, more shot through with sights and sounds and smells, and Ifan himself emerges as something akin to human. The novel is hampered throughout, however, by the self-satisfied, antiseptic Wales of the first part. It would appear that the ideal Wales has catered for everything except the expression of human will.

Accusations of propaganda had been levelled at CYSGOD Y CRYMAN. The merit of WYTHNOS YNG

NGHYMRU FYDD was that Islwyn Ffowc Elis disciplined himself never to write so unsubtly again.

A far more convincing evocation of the dystopian and the utopian visions of Wales, played out simultaneously against the backdrop of a scattered community in Powys, is found in BLAS Y CYNFYD (*A Taste of Prehistory*, 1958), the perfect antidote to WYTHNOS YNG NGHYMRU FYDD's high-mindedness. Written originally as a radio series, the novel shows Islwyn Ffowc Elis doing what he does best: telling a gripping story and suffusing it with wider significance. The story is developed with poise, the characterization is varied and credible, and the dialogue reads easily. Interior monologues and action are married with skill. In BLAS Y CYNFYD, Islwyn Ffowc Elis probably comes closest to achieving his self-declared aim of writing the 'pot-boiler', of which he had written a year before, with no pretence at being great literature. It has a solidity which makes it, if not his best novel, then arguably his most entertaining.

The title of the work echoes the words of R. Williams Parry's lyric, 'Eifionydd', a hymn of praise to the rural delights of *a place between mountain and sea* untouched by *the ugliness of Progress* in his own industrial valley:

>*Draw o ymryson ynfyd*
>*Chwerw'r newyddfyd blin,*
>*Mae yno flas y cynfyd*
>*Yn aros fel hen win.*

>(Away from the senseless, bitter striving
>Of the restless modern world,
>The taste of prehistory
>Lingers like vintage wine.)

The title is in part ironic. BLAS Y CYNFYD calls into question the rural idyll of CYSGOD Y CRYMAN by having at its centre an exiled Welshman, Elwyn Prydderch, whose own memories of his upbringing have been dimmed and gilded by twenty unbroken years in London. Neurotic, distressed and stifled by the crowds on the underground, Elwyn takes a month's leave in his native Cwm Bedw, certain that the countryside will restore him. He escapes his urban hell to find a world poised on a paradox: *the inexplicable strangeness of an old familiarity*. He is at once tourist and native, forgetful but not forgotten. His stay there becomes a journey into himself.

The narrative drive is provided by a mystery in Elwyn's own past. Why did his father leave Cwm Bedw for England? A story of violence, jealousy, double-dealing and resentment emerges, entangled still further by Elwyn's attraction to Llinos, the daughter of the villain, Wil Bowen.

A less scrupulous, less patient novelist would have entitled the book ANWIREDDAU'R TADAU (*The Sins of the Fathers*). The chosen title fixes the reader's mind on the social dimension of the work. Smuggled into the narrative is an extended examination of the narrow line between belonging and not belonging, to family and home, and to one's own past. In the eighth chapter, from which the book takes its name, the self-educated Caleb Morris, ninety-five and too much of a reader to have been any success as a farmer, gives Elwyn a lecture on the link between social cohesion and mental well-being:

*Do you know why neurosis is so common? . . . Individualism, which appeared to us to be such a good thing eighty years ago, has become corrupted. Run wild. Man has cut himself off from his neighbour and his roots. I suppose that you never think about your grandfather and grandmother. And do you have anything to do with your cousins, not to mention your second cousins and third cousins?*

The words for second and third cousins – 'ceifn' and 'gorcheifn' – are unfamiliar to Elwyn, as they no doubt would be for nine out of every ten readers. Caleb goes on:

*It was hard for the old Welsh. They lived on the verge of starvation, under the heel of lord and nobleman and landowner, with not enough clothes to wear and without a secure roof over their heads. But they weren't neurotic. They were too busy struggling to live. And they belonged. Do you understand? Belonged . . . You need something to grab hold of, my boy. Or something to wrap around yourself. You need to see yourself, not as a poor, lost, erring man, but as part of something greater than yourself.*

As has been seen, the epiphanies in Islwyn Ffowc Elis are often not of the main characters' making. Self-knowledge needs a nudge. Caleb Morris is pure Islwyn Ffowc: a character conjured up solely to deliver a speech upon which the direction of the book will turn. One is reminded of Maldwyn Edwards in YN ÔL I LEIFIOR, or FFENESTRI TUA'R GWYLL's Sirian Owen. Caleb Morris is a functional character whose appearance is confined to this chapter. He did not appear in the original radio script from which the novel was adapted. The author, however, takes pains to sketch him out, give him a history and a face, a family and interests. He carries a weight of authority built in a few pages. The touch is unobtrusive when compared, for example, with the set-piece homily on village life delivered by Hywel in WYTHNOS YNG NGHYMRU FYDD:

> Many sociologists felt that society was coming apart, and that individuals were coming apart as a result. Everyone keeping his home and his pleasures and his religion (if he had one) separate. And an attempt was made to bring everything together. Here, instead of the factory being a mile or more from the village, it's in the village centre, and the church and the social centre are in the same group of buildings.

The comparison points out a further shortcoming in WYTHNOS YNG NGHYMRU FYDD which is absent here: the smugness which underpins the earlier work is replaced by a storyline which contents itself with keeping the reader reading.

Cwm Bedw itself emerges as a character, though not quite Elwyn's half-imagined amalgam of long yellow summers and proper winters with *thick white snow, plenty of it, which stayed white until the very last day*. The place remains constant; its inhabitants change. The painful recognition of change is seen through Elwyn's eyes. The shop signs in the nearby market town are brasher than he remembers them, the traffic denser. The children on the school bus home to Llanfihangel Eryddon don't speak Welsh. Elwyn's own Welsh, we later learn, is considered foreign in its purity: the local shopkeeper takes him for a native of Anglesey or Merioneth. His relationship with Llinos develops hand-in-hand with an acceptance that time has altered him and his home to an equal degree. Elwyn's disenchantment with aspects of Cwm Bedw is counterbalanced by a rarer discovery. He has arrived in *a primitive society, perhaps. Basic too. And cruel. But there was no doubt that it was a society.*

Elwyn's guides on his journey into his past are Tomos and Elin Gruffydd, with whom he stays after fleeing the clutches of Menna, landlady of the Eryddon Arms, and Llinos herself. Tomos is the voice of reason and sanity, able to rationalize Wil Bowen to Elwyn as *any one of us but for the grace of God*. The story which emerges is a tale of lust and double-dealing. Elwyn's father, it transpires, was forced to leave Cwm Bedw after a fight in which Wil lost an eye. It was not, as Wil Bowen has maintained, the result of an argument over straying sheep, but the accidental consequence of his father fighting for Elwyn's sister's honour. The novel ends, in Tomos's words, with one of *those consecrated minutes in life, when years of confusion finally fall into some kind of order*. Elwyn settles in Cwm Bedw, repairing a break with the family history which should never have happened. Continuity is restored. One is reminded of the sunset on the Vaughan coat-of-arms at the end of CYSGOD Y CRYMAN.

Part whodunnit (or whydunnit), part love story, part social commentary and part romantic quest, BLAS Y CYNFYD is a rag-bag of genres which miraculously holds together. The story fits the space allotted to it like an apple fits its skin. The ending, where Elwyn marries Llinos and settles back into his old home, is contrived but somehow fitting in a novel obsessed with roots, rediscovery and reconciliation.

BLAS Y CYNFYD, moreover, provided Islwyn Ffowc Elis with the tensions between 'modern' and 'primitive', rooted and rootless, which were to feature in his later fiction, where *the strangeness of old familiarity* would reverberate in unexpected ways. His novels thereafter would be exercises in invasion and social disorientation, mapping the margins between civilization and mere anarchy. In so doing he would attempt what no novelist writing in Welsh had done: to give his readership the vicarious experience of seeing themselves as others saw them.

Islwyn Ffowc Elis's first vehicle was the satirical TABYRDDAU'R BABONGO (*The Drums of the Babongo*, 1961), where the colonial experience, lived out first as history, is relived as farce in an extended joke of the have-you-heard-the-one-about type. *In terms of craft*, Islwyn Ffowc Elis told one interviewer, *I believe that it was the tidiest novel I have written.*

It is also his most ironic. Its determinism pre-empts any po-faced criticism of racial stereotypes by making race the central issue. Its central character, Cadwaladr Ifans, is a myopic, teetotal Calvinist, *a thirty-five-year-old cherub with glasses and false teeth,* sent out to Black Africa to spread the civilizing virtues of the British Empire, who spreads chaos instead. He finds the pure physicality of the switch to Mbonga disconcerting:

*Black men were lovely in the overseas mission's film-strips and deserved a half-crown in the collection, poor souls. But being here in their midst . . . was an alarmingly different matter. Were the creatures safe?*

The journey becomes a nightmare of broken telephones, crowded trains and unintelligible voices. Cwm Bedw has nothing on this distant corner of the empire for ancient fears. Conrad meets Evelyn Waugh:

*The African night was wrapping them in its lap. There was nothing to see to left or right but the shadows of trees bent double like hags, and the long grass blowing as the wind from the jeep whipped it. The feeble light of the station was far behind them, and the torches of the native village winked like so many jack-o'-lanterns in the blackness. Above, the huge yellow stars of Africa stared down like the numberless eyes of some Being who refused to believe that white men were foolish enough to leave electricity and tap water behind.*

The journey from Mbonga to the plantation at Mbongo, his intended home for the next five years, takes five full chapters; plenty of time to sketch in a family background strangely similar to that of Elwyn Prydderch in BLAS Y CYNFYD. Cadwaladr, Dwalad, is a London Welshman, nostalgic for the family farm at Ty'n Rhos. The novel is interspersed with letters home to his family, explaining away his chequered career as a meteoric rise to new responsibilities and successes. At Mbongo he meets the historical accident of Britishness in the form of Talbot, a five-feet-five Englishman, the dour, alcoholic Macgregor, a man whose gestures and features seem to be composed entirely of rectangles with an equally rigid theology to match, and the libertine Irishman, O'Kelly.

The recurring irony of the book is that these agents of imperialism are less convinced than Ifans of the virtues of what they do. Talbot, in a rare departure from barking Telegraphese, asserts that there is no merit in turning Africans into second-hand Europeans:

*They don't want our religion or our education or our soap and water. They were a lot happier before we came here. But, since we are here, we must make the best of a bad job and change them as little as we can.*

Macgregor, more effusive and embittered, *past being disheartened long since*, has chosen Africa as a flight from the 'technological nightmare' of the West. A disciple of Rousseau, he cherishes savagery and fears that progress has set the African on the road to materialism and worse: *a washing machine to wreck his shirts, a mangle to smash his fingers. And a new set of illnesses like thrombosis, neurosis and every other osis.*

Ifans is a bundle of repressions, unsure of etiquette, keen on founding a Purity and Morality Society, haunted by vague sexual stirrings for Talbot's wife. His chapel upbringing has given him a conscience but no grace, in either the theological or social sense. He lacks what Macgregor defines as *common sense peppered with unaffectedness and salted with a sense of humour.* His life is a series of 'pratfalls' and misunderstandings, a one-man Whitehall farce.

The action of the novel is played out against the vague threat of native rebellion, fuelled by rumour. Jarmodo Mbawa, a Cambridge-educated constitutional nationalist, addresses rallies in the capital city; the native whites, as much victims of British imperialism as the blacks, are caught in the middle. In Mbongo, Talbot tells Cadwaladr, all stories are true. According to O'Kelly, everyone there remembers everything. Oppressed nations like their heroes to be mythic. Through a mixture of misunderstandings and wilful interpretation on the part of the natives, the determinedly unheroic Cadwaladr finds himself hailed as a potential national saviour by the Babongo, *a man from the north-lands, his skin the colour of the pebbles in the rivers and his language different from that of the white master or the black servant.*

Jarmodo is eclipsed. Cadwaladr undergoes the traditional trials by ordeal expected of the son of prophecy before being rescued from the uppermost branches of a tree by the story's love interest, Olwen Preese.

Cadwaladr returns to Britain. *Perhaps what you had in Africa*, Olwen suggests in the closing chapter, *was a kind of practice. Perhaps your fate lies in Wales . . . You could free your own people, the Welsh*. Cadwaladr is unconvinced, British to the last:

'Don't talk nonsense, Olwen. They're white people. They don't want freedom.'
'Perhaps they need it nonetheless.'

Although she almost immediately dismisses the idea as absurd, preferring to think of Dwalad as a perfect assistant preacher – *an outlet for your bad temper which would keep you respectable at the same time* – the point has been made: what Wales wants and what Wales needs are not necessarily the same thing.

Olwen's words are a barbed case for nationalism, an appeal to the head in the same way that the nameless, dying woman in WYTHNOS YNG NGHYMRU FYDD had been an appeal to the heart. They can be interpreted, too, as an implicit comment on the motivation behind the work in which they appear. A conflict between want and need had coloured Islwyn Ffowc Elis's approach to fiction from the outset; his work had always sought as much to teach as to entertain, although the emphasis had varied slightly from book to book. CYSGOD Y CRYMAN had reflected Islwyn Ffowc Elis's exuberant love of the form, and his *post hoc* justification of popular fiction as something *which in some strange way might save the language* was a bonus. FFENESTRI TUA'R GWYLL had been a pardonable self-indulgence, an experiment which served to confirm him in his adherence to the popular. YN ÔL I LEIFIOR balanced the desire to supply with audience demand. In WYTHNOS YNG NGHYMRU FYDD the propaganda which some had discerned in his earlier work was given almost cathartic expression. BLAS Y CYNFYD took the rural novel and tweaked it, introducing elements of savagery, predatory sex and mental instability. TABYRDDAU'R BABONGO, consciously set outside the familiar world of rural Welsh Wales, was an exercise in stretching the boundaries of Welsh fiction in respect of both technique and content.

For one thing, the perennial problem of how to write for English-speaking characters was overcome. CYSGOD Y CRYMAN had been criticized for the amount of English it contained, one critic (not wholly kindly) referring to it as *the first bilingual novel in Wales*. Later novels had glossed dialogue with parenthetical comments on the language used. By TABYRDDAU'R BABONGO the language is simply not an issue: the characters for the most part speak English; the novelist conveys the conversations in Welsh; the reader suspends disbelief and lets the narrative do the work. English is used sparingly, rendered in Welsh orthography and is generally used for comic effect. Islwyn Ffowc Elis, who had shown himself so capable of writing classically correct Welsh in CYN OERI'R GWAED, makes a virtue of linguistic bastardization.

As regards content, TABYRDDAU'R BABONGO raised the question: Is it possible for prose fiction in Welsh not to be Welsh in character? Can it be *Cymraeg* without being *Cymreig*? By 1961, the same year in which the novel was published, Islwyn Ffowc Elis was trying obliquely to come to terms with the idea, scenting already the difficulties inherent in writing for an audience who admired his work but found itself increasingly uncomfortable with the moral universe he was creating. His essay on 'Y Nofelydd a'i Gymdeithas' (*The Novelist and His Society*), published in the first issue of TALIESIN in the same year, is a key text, both a defence of the craft of the writer and a veiled assault on an audience who knew him all too well. In it he called every novelist *a bundle of prejudices*, incapable of objectivity:

*He may recognize some of his prejudices as prejudices, and repress them . . . As for the rest, they will not be his personal prejudices, but the acknowledged standards and preconceptions of his time and society, and he isn't likely to interfere too much with those in case he upsets his audience.*

The trouble was, he implied, that there was a growing discrepancy between those standards and preconceptions and his own ambitions as a novelist. He used the essay to state what he called another truth:

*Not only is every novelist conditioned by the society in which he was raised; his work is conditioned by the audience for which he writes.*

An acute sense of audience had fuelled both Islwyn Ffowc Elis's desire to write and the success he had enjoyed. A decade later, this same sense now constrained him. The topic of sex, he wrote, typified the restrictions under which Welsh novelists were obliged to work:

> In very few Welsh novels, even recent ones, is there an account of the physical relationship between a man and a woman or a boy and a girl. I am ready enough to accept that any number of Welsh novelists may have little interest in this, or may feel perhaps that they lack the technique to treat such material in a literary way. But I also know that the objection to descriptions of sex is still so strong in Welsh society as to make novelists avoid the subject, or at least handle it with extreme caution.

One suspects that for Islwyn Ffowc Elis sex was more than the 'convenient example' he claims it to be here. A study of sexual sublimation in his early fiction could be whisked up into a worthy if repetitive postgraduate thesis. Harri Vaughan is torn first between the virginal Lisabeth and the temptress Gwylan, then re-enacts the dilemma with Marged and Vera. Ceridwen Morgan's frustrations find an outlet in literature and manic coquetry. Karl and Greta subsume their desires in piety and politics respectively. Elwyn Prydderch and Cadwaladr display potentially tragic and blackly comic facets of the same repression.

The more general point, however, was well made: Islwyn Ffowc Elis felt compromised by the very expectations which had first induced him to write. Writing social fiction *yn Gymraeg* required writing *yn Gymreig*, with all its intrinsic impediments. The realization precipitated an artistic crisis. He would not write another extended piece of prose fiction for seven years. In 1963, he turned his back on full-time writing, left north Wales and, aged nearly forty, began a new career.

# IV

In an unpublished account of the events leading up to this literary stagnation, Islwyn Ffowc Elis suggests that his true creative period only ran for the ten years between 1951 and 1961. Born out of youthful enthusiasm, made necessary in different ways by difficult personal circumstances within the ministry and, thereafter, by the brave decision to freelance, his work had by the early 1960s gathered a momentum and a confidence.

This momentum was stopped dead, this confidence shattered, by a combination of factors. First, there was the understandable, if destructive, concern of friends and relatives that full-time writing in Welsh was not possible. Second, Islwyn Ffowc Elis's decision to contest Montgomery for Plaid Cymru in May 1962 caused the postponement of the television series RHAI YN FUGEILIAID (*Some Shepherds Abiding*) under the Representation of the People Act, precipitating an unfounded concern, after months of delay, that the BBC had lost interest in his work.

Artistic self-doubt was exacerbated by the decision to take a lectureship at Trinity College, Carmarthen, early in 1963. For three months, during which Islwyn Ffowc Elis was obliged to prepare between fifteen and eighteen hours of lectures a week, the family was effectively homeless. Eventually they were panicked into buying a house in Llansteffan, eight miles from the college. It was to be their home for the next two years, during which Islwyn Ffowc Elis managed to complete just one short story.

Ironically, with a regular salary assured, invitations began to arrive: a commission for another television drama series, GWANWYN DIWEDDAR (*Late Spring*, 1963), a pageant, a radio series called IMPROVE YOUR WELSH, and a continuing regular monthly column for the current affairs magazine, BARN. Feeling unable to refuse, Islwyn Ffowc Elis postponed the work for which he felt a passion. Life in Carmarthen became a curious rerun of the petty frustrations which had made his time in the ministry so uncongenial, with the, to him inexplicable, difference that whereas the ministry had spurred him creatively, Trinity College induced self-pitying inertia.

Two reasons for the difference immediately suggest themselves, both deriving from the simple fact that Islwyn Ffowc Elis was ten years older. His early work had been prompted at least in some degree by a desire to make a name for himself. During the course of the 1950s the thrill of seeing his name in print had inevitably diminished. In a broader sense, too, the satisfaction of composing, editing and completing a piece of creative fiction is governed by the same law of diminishing returns. Coupled with this was an unexpressed awareness that the dynamic of the relationship between writing and 'real work' had been reversed. Writing had been an escape from his perceived failings as a minister; Carmarthen in its turn had become an escape from his perceived inability to survive as a writer. From the beginning, his appointment there was coloured by a tacit concession that what had preceded it was of questionable value. It represented, at least in part, a self-imposed challenge to his identity.

A third possible explanation is that the novel was no longer the best medium for the increasingly introspective nature of his work. In several important respects, despite – indeed, because of its playful elements – TABYRDDAU'R BABONGO can be seen as a more embittered reworking of FFENESTRI TUA'R GWYLL. Islwyn Ffowc Elis's decision to locate it in Africa, with its western literary heritage of menace and suspicion, exile and mutual incomprehension, is significant. It depicts an unnatural, necessarily temporary society in upheaval. Its comedy is bleak, to say the least, and Islwyn Ffowc Elis has the talent to make the reader uncomfortably complicit. All the more so now that critical anachronism has led to charges of racism and sexism. It is, in truth, a profoundly ironic piece. In Cadwaladr, Islwyn Ffowc Elis creates a character whose shortcomings are obvious to everyone but himself, and our best efforts to like him are undermined throughout by a less worthy but somehow more urgent desire to see him make a fool of himself. And Cadwaladr does little to help his own cause. His acts of self-assertion are clumsy but exploitative, such as the attempted seductions of Mrs Talbot and, later, Olwen. There are moments of physical cruelty, too, when these cartoon creations spill real blood. A plantation worker is caught under a tree and squeals like a stuck pig to the general indifference of the overseers; Cadwaladr whips the plantation workers in a curious act of fear described by the author as *understandable but unfortunate*, and is beaten in his turn by Talbot. Socially, too, the work has the self-absorbed feel of a short story: hell is other people. Quite simply, the characters are bored with one another, with the limitations their surroundings force upon them, and with the lives that led them to this God-forsaken corner of the empire in the first place. TABYRDDAU'R BABONGO is a gathering of grotesques, a repository for personalities without the qualities to live in their own societies and by extension the depth of character to survive in any of Islwyn Ffowc Elis's other novels.

A fourth reason for Islwyn Ffowc Elis's inability to write a novel, already alluded to in the previous chapter, is pertinent here, too. By the time of his move to Carmarthen he had already admitted to himself that a writer in Welsh was bound by the moral standards of his audience. Although TABYRDD-AU'R BABONGO challenged that assumption, with hindsight it is not difficult to see it as a retreat. Perhaps, too, Islwyn Ffowc Elis's obligation to his audience extended to setting as much as to content, and his original creative instinct to combine comfortable entertainment with a desire to teach, to write about the rural communities he knew and with which the huge majority of his readers were familiar, or for which they generally had an affection, had been the right one. This was his natural constituency, like Kate Roberts's and T. Rowland Hughes's rural Arfon or D. J. Williams's corner of north Carmarthenshire. Topographically, if not technically, Islwyn Ffowc Elis might be considered to have overreached himself in setting a lone Welshman in the African outback.

It was Islwyn Ffowc Elis's misfortune, he claims, not to have learned to view writing as a craft which demands self-discipline. The ease with which he had written his early work – *an inability not to write*, as he put it – had left him without the resources to write despite himself when the direction in which he wanted to go was unclear. It was a case-study in writer's block, where uncertainty about content combined with paralysing self-criticism to produce stasis. Loss of self-confidence feeds on itself. So sensitive was Islwyn Ffowc Elis by the mid-1960s, that an apparently innocuous factual mistake in the WESTERN MAIL concerning a novel in progress about Gruffudd ap Llywelyn for which he had received a bursary of £1,500 from the Welsh Arts Council (the elements in the main character's name were reversed) caused him to abandon the work with 30,000 words completed. When Islwyn Ffowc Elis made his application for a Readership at Lampeter in 1983, the novel was still described as 'work in progress'.

A final, tentative explanation derives from Islwyn Ffowc Elis's admiration for and championing of Tegla Davies (1880–1967), first as editor of the *festschrift*, EDWARD TEGLA DAVIES: LLENOR A PHROFFWYD (*Edward Tegla Davies: Writer and Prophet*, 1956), as guest lecturer on DIRGELWCH TEGLA (*The Mystery of Tegla*) at the 1977 Wrexham Eisteddfod and in numerous other shorter pieces.

Tegla's literary career in some respects mirrors Islwyn Ffowc Elis's own a generation and a half later. Both were ministers, both sought to write popular, accessible literature and both enjoyed early critical acclaim. In the case of the former, this proved short-lived. In his Wrexham lecture, Islwyn Ffowc Elis implies an academic conspiracy to account for this:

> *There are several reasons, I am sure, why Tegla has slipped the attention of contemporary literary criticism. But I must comment on one, although it is painful for me. Some time in the twenties some people decided, perhaps under the leadership of someone, that this non-graduate, uneducated author, who was a Wesleyan minister of all things, was far too popular and was receiving too much praise, and that it was time to silence the acclaim.*

There is at least half a case for arguing that Islwyn Ffowc Elis's own literary retreat as he, like Tegla before him, moved towards early middle-age was in part an unconscious attempt to anticipate his own loss of popularity through self-imposed silence. Islwyn Ffowc Elis, sufficiently sensitive to criticism that not only did he write FFENESTRI TUA'R GWYLL *for the critics*, but followed this up with a public apology for its unpopularity, did not want to suffer a similar fate. To become unfashionable was bad enough; to have unfashionability thrust upon him by a cabal was insupportable.

The results of this sense of failure which overcame Islwyn Ffowc Elis, whatever its cause, are dissected in the short story 'Hunandosturi' (*Self-Pity*, 1973), which closes the collection of eleven pieces in MARWYDOS (*Embers*, 1974). The story begins with an ending: *It was finished*. Middle-aged Ieuan completes his latest, unnamed novel, but is unhappy with it. He will not send it to his publishers because it doesn't deserve to be published. It is the product *of a writer who has been and gone*. He no longer feels the sense of achievement and release which a successfully completed project used to bring:

> *That old euphoria when work was finished, the knots tied, a pile*

*of creativity off-loaded onto a mound of paper and the knowledge that it was alive and entertaining and captivating although it wouldn't please everyone . . . the euphoria that would never return.*

The novel, he explains to Esyllt, his wife, is *stone dead . . . sixty thousand leaden words screwed together.* In its author's mind the stillborn creation grows into a metaphor for his failing creative powers, retribution for his early popularity, a reminder of unfulfilled promise and an image of his own impending mortality. He is the victim of others' expectations, a popular writer who despises his own work and, by extension, his own readership. His wife argues a case which he himself may once have argued: to write in Welsh is an obligation. For the politically naïve Mrs Williams, a neighbour – who regards road signs and a Welsh-language television channel as irrelevant, who answers the phone and writes cheques in English – his books are *a tiny wire which connects her and thousands like her to things Welsh, and it would be a disaster to break it.* The truth, however, is that the fine wire which connects him with the next generation is fraying, too. His daughter Bethan shows literary talent, but makes light of it:

'*Dad, can I preach for a minute?*'
'*Well?*'
'*First. By the time I reach the age you are now, not many people will be able to read. Everything will be signs and symbols and figures, and everyone will have a little radar box in his chest to sense everyone else's thoughts. There won't even be any need for language –*'
'*Where on earth did you get those crazy ideas –?*'
'*Second.*' *She was merciless.* '*Even if people could read, do you think I'd be stupid enough to shut myself in some dusty study all day and scribble? And starve for my trouble? I'll do*

*my best in school so that – as you're always saying – I can get something better afterwards. But it won't be writing . . . Oh, I'll do all I can to keep The Language – for as long as language is needed. I might well go to prison for it. But I'm not going to half starve writing to keep it, and worry myself sick.'*

A similar desolation informs the *skeleton of a novel*, first published in 1969, which gives the volume its title. The story, although set a generation earlier, is tantalizingly autobiographical. Again, it opens when the battle is lost. We are presented with, rather than introduced to, Owain Box Humphrys, once a genius, now a broken man. *The storms of life had bombarded his brain cells into smithereens.* An only child, Owen (as he was christened) had been able to speak at eighteen months, read at three, write at four and was composing verse before his sixth birthday. His genius is an inconvenience to his bourgeois family. Their respectability and his innate passivity conspire to destroy him. *Condemned never to say 'No'* because of guilt about his feelings of love towards his mother, he resigns himself to entering the ministry:

*Since he could not stand on his own two feet he would lean on the eternal arms. The ambition of the pulpit was a pure ambition: authority without guilt; ability without shame . . . His self-deception was as yet too young to be hypocrisy.*

*In deciding to enter the ministry he was submitting to the desire of his family. But that was incidental. Owen was certain – very certain – that it was his own choice, or better still, that it was the choice of Providence.*

The change in voice from Owain's own self-justification to authorial comment is significant. Islwyn Ffowc Elis the writer dogs the footsteps of his creation throughout, providing a running commentary on a life very much like his own, but gifted with hindsight which lends irony to the narrative. The story, indeed, is a deliberate confusion of genres and devices: a condensed novel (itself an implicit admission on the author's part of his inability to write the real thing) interspersed with diary entries, a mock review, a couple of lines from an interview with the author, exposition, time-shifts, direct petitions to the reader on Owain's behalf, the occasional *moment of psychologizing* and techniques which deliberately prevent readers from identifying too closely with the subject, or even with the author himself.

*But let us continue with our story*, Islwyn Ffowc Elis writes. For Owain, college provides *the first sweet explosion in his life*. He gains a girlfriend, embraces socialism, writes poetry and Welshifies his name. A poor degree hardly seems to matter.

Married to Mary, who is *blindly loyal to her husband*, Owain embarks on his first post as minister at Bethany, where the damp in the walls is accepted by the deacons as the will of God but Owain's suggestion to set up a drama group is condemned as a sin against the Holy Spirit. His allegiance to Labour upsets his Liberal flock. He can't preach, lacks the prosaic patience to make small talk. He loses himself in literature, *squeezing his work out of himself like toothpaste is squeezed from a tube*.

A failed political career follows, part-time lecturing and the slow decline into a life with so little incident that it doesn't merit attention. The end of the body of the story is non-committal:

*Perhaps there will be a lot of theorizing about what happened to*

*Owain Box. And perhaps there won't be. But some will continue to say that he was once a genius.*

What might be called the more conventional short stories in the collection also pursue the ideas of finality and decline. The viewpoint is always retrospective. In 'Oedfa Tomos Wiliam' (*Thomas Wiliam's Service*, 1960) a stubborn chapel-goer refuses to acknowledge that the pillar of his life has been taken from him. A country station accepts the Beeching axe in 'Y Trên Olaf' (*The Last Train*, 1963). Local boy made good Marty Jones in 'Seren Unnos' (*One-time Star*, 1968) sacrifices his roots for a brief career as a recording artist peddling second-hand sentiment. William Jones in 'Cymwynas' (*A Favour*, 1960 and rewritten in 1973) goes to his grave believing himself responsible for the death of a friend.

There are also stories which reveal an absurdist streak. 'Gryffis', dating from 1949, tells the story of a brief encounter between a shopkeeper and the eponymous hero. Gryffis returns to his native patch, although nobody remembers him, criticizes the anglicization of the area in a torrent of Wenglish, calls the shopkeeper a liar for putting the name Evans on his sign when his face clearly shows him to be a Jones, and leaves a scribbled cheque for £2,500.

Equally eccentric is Wil in 'Y Polyn' (*Song of a Pole*, 1967, which appeared in the author's own English translation in Oxford University Press's WELSH SHORT STORIES in 1971). Wil has an obsession with a newly-erected telegraph pole. It has no meaning for him other than its own innate beauty *'People are very stupid to worry about money and food,'* he tells the story's narrator in the Christ-like tones of a holy fool.

'This pole toils not neither does it spin, yet it can sing like faith.' Egging one another on in a *folie à deux*, the two men decide to unearth the pole and move it. It is a gratuitous act which will, in Wil's words,

smash the pile of prejudices which were wrapped around you with the blankets of your cot, and give you a brand new pile in their place.

The project proceeds, gradually attracting onlookers – a postman, a policeman, the local surveyor and two passing Englishmen – to lend a hand until realization dawns and the authorities are informed:

The court was merciful. Or so people say locally, at least. Wil and I were given a fine of two pounds each, plus costs, and an order for Wil to see a specialist to have his head examined. The knowledgeable chap concluded that there was a touch of schizophrenia or paranoia or megalomania or one of those long words which quieten the mind of civilization . . .

But some nights, when the sky is clear and the moon is full, Wil and I go to give the pole a cuddle. I sit with my legs astride its base and look up along its shining length until the moon is slap above it and feel that I have married the light. And Wil starts to dream. And his voice once again turns me into a heap of sweet paralysis.

A summary inevitably strips the story of its sense of fun. There is a sense here of a community which tolerates eccentricity and a delight in the playfulness of obsession. Although Islwyn Ffowc Elis has been publicly dismissive of the short story (confessing in the foreword to MARWYDOS that he had published only a couple of dozen over a period of thirty years and had forgotten some of them completely), the form is liberating, allowing him to exercise a weary knowingness, almost a cynicism, which he had denied to himself in his preferred vehicle of the novel since FFENESTRI TUA'R GWYLL.

One story deserves special mention. 'Ar Fôr Tymhestlog' (*On a Stormy Sea*, 1971) takes its title from a nineteenth-century hymn expressing faith in the teeth of adversity. Its canvas is an afternoon and evening in the life of a harassed schoolteacher, Arthur Lewis. This Arthur's heroism is to survive at all. Neighbours engage him in malicious gossip, his son scalds himself with boiling water, his wife is a shrew, bureaucracy frustrates him, his head considers him ineffectual and his pupils consider him a figure of fun. Islwyn Ffowc Elis's triumph is not to interpret, not to explain: merely to allow the reader – through scatter-gun dialogue and occasional interior monologues – to live alongside this unremarkable, patient and fundamentally decent man for five thousand words or so. This technical restraint results in one of Islwyn Ffowc Elis's most sympathetic creations.

Islwyn Ffowc Elis allows himself to break with the restriction for one magnificently comic paragraph. Arthur, plagued by Mr Jones next door for the loan of a rake, finally surrenders to a fit of suburban catharsis. The present tense adds to the effect:

*Arthur marches through to the tool-shed. Arthur grabs hold of the rake. Arthur carries it to the wall and hurls it like a fiery spear into the middle of Mr Jones next door's begonias. And suddenly, Arthur feels better.*

The day ends with Arthur in bed, clinging to the sleeping form of his wife, revelling in a tunnel of forgetfulness before another day dawns, *resplendent with greater and better troubles.*

Islwyn Ffowc Elis's return to novel-writing, Y BLANED DIRION (*The Gentle Planet*, 1968), began life as a radio drama serial in 1959 and its genesis can be still be discerned in its reliance on voice and dramatic plot developments at the end of chapters. As science fiction, it has inevitably dated; as an experiment in cosmic theology, it still makes an intriguing read.

The narrative is, on the face of it, confusingly layered. The body of the text purports to be a journal found in a space capsule by the American military, sent to Wales for translation and recast as fiction by its anonymous translator when its contents are suppressed for security reasons.

The book's characters are drawn from the stock casting of a hundred cinema matinées. Emrys and Elen have looks, youth, intelligence and mutual attraction to commend them: he an astronomer and she a brilliant, *uncomfortably attractive* anthropologist. The atmosphere between them fairly crackles with sexual electricity.

Elen's theories about the extraterrestrial origin of mankind are confirmed by an invitation to join a trip into outer space, by physicist Teyrnon Williams, a magus figure in the mould of WYTHNOS YNG NGHYMRU FYDD's Doctor Heinkel.

A team of six eventually make the trip: Emrys, Elen, Teyrnon, an Americanized business magnate, Owen D. Lewis, Captain Stevens as pilot and the ribald

Twm Sbanar, an engineer who *loves aeroplane engines so much that I could happily sleep with one of them every night*. Twm is without doubt Islwyn Ffowc Elis's most aggravating creation: tiresomely whimsical, fatuous and irrepressibly cheerful. We await his come-uppance with relish.

After a ponderous start, the story gathers pace at chapter 21, roughly half way through the narrative. 'Something providential' causes the ship to land on a planet, Theros, which sustains human life. Theros calls to mind the utopian Wales of the first part of WYTHNOS YNG NGHYMRU FYDD: beautiful, ordered but essentially forbidding. The atmosphere is *miraculous . . . like the air on the top of Berwyn or the Black Mountain on a fresh May morning*, the land is a living carpet and the sky is suffused with a pale blue light. The travellers enter a world set about with inverted commas, where the correspondence with what is familiar is tenuous. Their first hours there become an extended debate on whether the existence of God can be proved from design. As Twm Sbanar, in a rare fit of seriousness, puts it:

*There must be a God. If there isn't, I'd go mad here and now. He is the only thing now that can keep us attached to Earth.*

Eventually they meet an inhabitant, Araon, who becomes the visitors' guide to this Eden beyond the stars. As he tells them:

*Fear doesn't exist on the Gentle Planet . . . Life here is as it will be on your Earth in another thousand generations, when your leaders and your peoples have forgotten how to love and hate.*

But the visitors do love and hate. The God which

keeps them umbilical to Earth is a god built in their own imperfect image. They find perfection disorientating. As Teyrnon writes in his journal as the beauty palls: *The peace and the high moral atmosphere tend to enslave us, to belittle us.* Fundamental human desire reasserts itself. Elen falls in love with Araon, prompting a fit of jealousy from Emrys. Captain Stevens is overcome with greed for the abundant gold on the planet's surface; Twm raids the planet's museum for liquor and drifts into alcoholism; Lewis seeks the power which the planet's technology can give him. Even Teyrnon, until then the novel's moral compass, realizes that he has succumbed to pride in his own ability to stand aloof from temptation. Worse still, their deviant behaviour sets in train a 'virus' of anarchy among the planet's inhabitants. In a scene reminiscent of a 1960s American campus under the sway of Timothy Leary, the planet's youth tune in, turn on and drop out, making a Lord of Misrule figure out of Twm Sbanar.

Our tarnished heroes escape. Teyrnon's journal, kept in Welsh as an act of courage, tells the tale of this cosmic Scott, a man who dies because the ambition within him has been killed by his encounter with a perfection which is beyond him. Around him, the crew are lost in the silence of their own regrets. Their craft pitches into the Pacific Ocean and they perish.

Where Y BLANED DIRION excels in comparison with, say, WYTHNOS YNG NGHYMRU FYDD is that it makes the examination of an alien culture a mirror which reflects a wider view of human nature. Perfection, it tells us, destroys the value of means by which we seek to attain it. Its successful pursuit consists in the submission of the will, in surrendering love, communication, artistic endeavour and even the prospect of death. It means denying the self to a degree which makes its enjoyment logically impossible. Whether or not there is any truth in Islwyn Ffowc Elis's claim that the novel would have been a better one had it been written ten years earlier, it still has an honourable place in the canon because in a fuller sense Teyrnon and his crew are metaphors for the characters in all fiction who are motivated by desire for a perfection which would ultimately be self-destructive. The novel is a reminder that 'perfection' is derived from the concept of completion. The Gentle Planet is a place without stories, because stories arise from conflict. It is where Greta and Karl or Elwyn and Llinos will spend their married lives; where Cadwaladr and Olwen will disembark at the end of their journey out of Africa; the Wales where Ifan Powel will see the fruits of his political education.

Islwyn Ffowc Elis's career as a novelist ended with Y GROMLECH YN YR HAIDD (*Stones in the Barley*, 1970) and EIRA MAWR (*Whiteout*, 1971), both telling the story of the humbling of proud men. There is a certain irony in their having been written at all. Almost a generation after Islwyn Ffowc Elis sought to provide Wales with popular fiction, a scheme commissioned authors to produce that very same thing, and these two 40,000-word works were his contribution. Their author has been dismissive of both, as much because of their linear plots as anything. It is not difficult to read them as the purrs of a well-tuned narrative engine working at less than full efficiency.

Y GROMLECH YN YR HAIDD is part thriller, part

morality tale, expanding on themes hinted at in BLAS Y CYNFYD. Bill Henderson, the stubborn English owner of Hendre, roots up a set of standing stones on his land in the interests of modernization and suffers the retribution of ancient powers for his trouble. The story follows the gradual decline of his fortune as each of the three stones is removed. Henderson's motivation is 'self-respect', a desire to make *Hendre look something like a farm and not like a piece of Connemara.* His utilitarianism will brook no opposition from superstitious peasants. Eventually, he infects the surrounding countryside with foot and mouth disease, loses his unborn child and becomes a haunted, jibbering wreck.

Well before the end, it becomes clear that Henderson himself is to be seen as a disease, the representative of a 'pitiable race', as local sage Benni Rees of Sychbant describes him:

*You know them. They're people who live in a glass ball. A ball which rolls from place to place, rolling from some colourless, shapeless town over there in England, only to roll back there some day, perhaps. They don't know what it is to stand still, and be still, under one constant light. The light changes, their view changes, they can't live without change, that's why the ball has to keep rolling.*

Continuity and change, the counterweights of CYN OERI'R GWAED and the source of the narrative energy of all Islwyn Ffowc Elis's significant fiction, are the stuff of his final novel, too. EIRA MAWR explores the restorative power of rural solitude. A throwaway novel by the author's own admission, it carries the themes of a longer, deeper work. The story opens with its central characters, Trefor and Diana, snowbound in the Berwyn mountains on a trip to Holyhead. The relationship between them is as cold and restrictive as the white mass that gathers around their car. Their fifteen-year marriage is virtually over; old jealousies have been rehearsed, old wounds fester. Although the story is set during the Big Freeze of 1947, we are looking in effect at what might have become of Greta and Paul Rushmere by the early 1970s: living in London; he weighed down by work and sustained by whisky; she a trapped animal, nostalgic for the simpler life they led when Trefor was a clerk and when they had time to be together. *I've got a laughing engine inside me, well-oiled for years*, she tells him, *and my face has become a piece of elastic which can smile at anyone who's important to you, whether I feel like it or not*.

In contrast, the farm where Huw and Meri Thomas have brought up their family is a place of light, warmth, security and unselfconscious sincerity. The home is run with *rule-of-thumb psychology* and attention to hygiene and good plain cooking. The children are introduced in turn: fifteen-year-old Bethan, the pretty Dilys and Wiliam, a born farmer in his father's mould.

The lives of these two disparate sets of people collide over the course of a week, when Trefor and Diana find themselves the reluctant guests of the Thomas family, 'buried alive', as Trefor puts it, in a smallholding without electricity, telephone or much of a concept of private space. The atmosphere of the piece is reminiscent of the spaceship in Y BLANED DIRION. Before the resurrection which this premature burial must occasion, all of them learn their different lessons.

While Huw and Meri hover like guardian angels – hospitable, resourceful and quietly competent – Wiliam has his prejudices about city types challenged. *My opinion is already formed*, he tells his family during his first appearance, in words that bring to mind Llinos Bowen's assertion in BLAS Y CYNFYD:

*There are two types of people. Cultured, hard-working country people, who have to earn their living in all weathers. And town people, made soft by too many conveniences and fripperies . . . And both types should live their own lives.*

By the book's close, he has learned an admiration for Trefor, but is confirmed in the value of his own way of life.

For Bethan, it is the awareness of the growing gap between herself and her older sister, a coming of age, an introduction to the intrigues of adult relationships. Her head spins with the romance of the Mabinogi and she develops a crush on Trefor, *such a beautiful, important and busy man*. Dilys, meanwhile, becomes aware of how attractive she is to Trefor, alarmed by the power and powerlessness this gives.

The focus of the book, however, is the salvation of Diana and Trefor's marriage. Diana's own conversion to simple pleasures is perhaps too glib to be convincing, the character too gifted with self-knowledge. By the first morning she is *enjoying herself enormously* in the unheated house with its single cold tap in the yard. *I want to savour every passing minute*, she tells her husband, looking at the white of the snow reflected on the wallpaper. By the end of the book, she has articulated the conversion more thoroughly still:

*It's wonderful to escape from a world where everything is so oppressively convenient. There's freedom here. Time doesn't weigh anyone down, there's no need to rush anywhere and everything is enough of a trouble to make you appreciate having it.*

Trefor, meanwhile, who claims to lose his self-respect when he misses his morning shave, a businessman who considers the FINANCIAL TIMES more valuable than breakfast, rediscovers the benefits of physical hard labour, learns a sense of proportion, and, as he looks out on the snow, becomes aware of his own mortality:

*A view to remember for ever. For a lifetime, rather, he corrected himself: a sun such as this one would light slopes like those long, long after our frail bodies have rotted into the earth.*

The novel reaches its climax in the shared enterprise of searching for lost sheep in a conifer plantation, *a snow temple*, where Trefor gives Dilys *a long, greedy kiss* in a scene which calls to mind Harri's brief fall from grace in YN ÔL I LEIFIOR. The action prompts him to go back to Diana. The snow conveniently melts the following day, allowing the guests to leave, their marriage saved.

Despite their faults, Y GROMLECH YN YR HAIDD and EIRA MAWR are important additions to the Islwyn Ffowc Elis canon, reiterating the author's concern with belonging, incursion and grace. In diluted form, they contain the staples of his better fiction: sage, rebel and pretty girl; remoteness and home; ambition and compromise. Taking the canon together, it is tempting to see something of the nineteenth-century actor-manager about him, allotting parts to his cast of favourite characters, changing the backdrop, asking for anger and tenderness as the script requires, and demanding nothing more of the audience than the imagination to suspend disbelief and a willingness to be entertained.

# V

Until recently, it was fashionable to speak in a Welsh context of a writer's 'contribution', his *cymwynas* or 'service', as if writing in Welsh in a bilingual country were by extension writing for the language, a case of *noblesse oblige*, an act of generosity, a hand dipped into the pocket when the collection plate is passed round for the welfare of a friend fallen on hard times. It was the climate in which Islwyn Ffowc Elis worked and which, more than anything, sets him apart from those who followed. An alteration in the social status of the language, the creation of a generation of professional media-orientated writers in Welsh, the continuing expansion of Welsh-medium education, a Welsh Language Board and a Welsh Language Act, have brought with them a consequent change in attitude. The idea of the committed and self-denying writer, hinted at by Islwyn Ffowc Elis in 1957, has been compromised by circumstances.

And no bad thing, too. The idea of a writer who makes a 'contribution' carries with it, for one thing, an uncomfortable implication of artistic relativism, or rather a confusion of roles. If the best that can be said of Islwyn Ffowc Elis half a century on from his début as an author is that he did his bit for the language – and this was said countless times with genuine gratitude by contemporary reviewers – then Welsh literary criticism needs to take a long look at itself. At this distance a more fruitful question to ask is what Islwyn Ffowc Elis's critical legacy has been. Is the Welsh novel in better shape for his involvement?

To answer the question requires us to place Islwyn Ffowc Elis's achievement in its historical context. In 1891, four years before his death, Daniel Owen looked forward in the preface to ENOC HUWS to the dawn of a Welsh literature which would owe more to George Eliot than to the mystic hymn-writer Ann Griffiths: the medium of that new literature would be the novel; its stage would be society rather than the recesses of the soul; its raw material the interaction of men rather than the communion of man and God; its voice would be more satirical than saintly; and the prodigal son rather than the saint would be its hero. Owen wrote:

*The history and customs of Wales, indeed Welsh life, have until now been virgin soil, and I am confident that presently we shall see the foremost writers of our land bringing what distinguishes us as a nation into this branch of literature.*

Owen, acute observer of human nature though he was, was spectacularly wrong. For two generations after his death, the novel was largely ignored. The onset of industrialization and urban living, with its consequent effect on the population and language balance of Wales, the decline in chapel culture and the establishment of a petty bourgeoisie, so cleverly caricatured in ENOC HUWS and seemingly so fruitful a field, proved inimical to the establishment of a tradition of fiction-writing in Welsh. Quite simply, Wales lacked the self-confidence to produce extended contemporary fiction, the conviction that Wales had stories to tell to herself and the willingness to acknowledge that there was literary mileage in a dying language. A collective and almost unconscious decision was made that the language couldn't take the artistic, social and moral risk of making itself a medium for the examination of change. Instead, popular literature contented itself with cheap verse endlessly retelling a myth of rural virtue, praising the toil-worn hands of mothers and the hearths of whitewashed cottages; and academic writers wrote introspective verse and essays. Small wonder, then, that the literary renaissance of the first half of the twentieth century produced little more than a dozen volumes of short stories. Where the desire to write extended prose fiction existed, it was constrained by lack of talent, lack of opportunity, perceived lack of public interest, or by the unwillingness of talented writers with a ready audience to identify themselves primarily as novelists. T. Gwynn Jones wrote two novels at the turn of the century, then turned to poetry; Saunders Lewis's MONICA (1931) was an exercise in Catholic piety, for which the author found a more amenable vehicle in drama; Kate Roberts wrote two short novels in the 1920s and the compressed epic TRAED MEWN CYFFION in 1936, but her first passion was the short story. Gwenallt's PLASAU'R BRENIN (1933), about his experiences as a conscientious objector during the Great War, was the result of a bet. T. Rowland Hughes, perhaps the nearest that Wales came to producing a recognized novelist, wrote as therapy for a terminal illness.

Islwyn Ffowc Elis's first achievement, then, was to identify himself as a novelist at all. His second was to see the stuff of literature – however populist – in a changing Wales. His third achievement was to confer status on the form as something legitimately Welsh.

Moreover, he created a readership for his work – unsophisticated originally, and certainly over-ready to praise – and grew with it, coaxing and cajoling it to demand and accept more. Islwyn Ffowc Elis, it would hardly be an overstatement to say, taught a generation of readers to read extended fiction in the language, and, as importantly, to think of Welsh as a suitable medium for such an enterprise.

It involved a reappraisal of both language and subject-matter. R. Gerallt Jones, in an afterword to Meic Stephens's 1998 translation of CYSGOD Y CRYMAN, observed that Islwyn Ffowc Elis created a style for the novel which broke with the prose rhythms of Bible-based Nonconformism. His idiom is a trick with rhetorical smoke and mirrors, making his work appear more expansive than it is, conjuring a train journey through Powys in a half-dozen sentences at the beginning of CYSGOD Y CRYMAN or the tedium of small-town isolation in a sweep of the bay as through a telescope in the opening paragraph of FFENESTRI TUA'R GWYLL, and leaving the afterimage of something greater on the story to follow.

The Wales he has chosen to write about, either directly, or in thinly veiled allegories, is a country which simultaneously entices and appals him. Quite literally, he loves Wales for all her faults. The characters in his novels have become extensions of that ambivalence: heroes and villains, naïvely drawn on occasions, but none the less compelling, an expression of Wales's enduring fascination for him.

This fascination, this questioning, sceptical love has been perhaps his greatest contribution of all. In a literature which has gained immeasurably in self-confidence over the last twenty-five years, but still exhibits a self-consciousness born of its minority status – where *Cymraeg* cannot be dissociated from *Cymreig* – his critical legacy has been the creation of a climate in which that self-consciousness is legitimized by deference to craft. It seems as well to end this examination where it began, with Islwyn Ffowc Elis's own words in 1957, the year in which his own literary self-confidence was at its greatest. He said then, anticipating the criticism which his work would receive:

*If he is a man of profound convictions, he has a right to express his convictions on the understanding that his work will not be judged in years to come on its worth as propaganda, but on how poorly or well his propaganda has been expressed.*

# A Select Bibliography

## ISLWYN FFOWC ELIS

*Creative Works*

Cyn Oeri'r Gwaed, Llandysul, Gwasg Gomer, 1952.

Cysgod y Cryman, Llandysul, Gwasg Gomer, 1953.

Ffenestri tua'r Gwyll, Llandysul, Gwasg Gomer, 1955.

Yn Ôl i Leifior, Llandysul, Gwasg Gomer, 1956.

Wythnos yng Nghymru Fydd, Caerdydd, Plaid Cymru, 1957.

Blas y Cynfyd, Llandysul, Gwasg Gomer, 1958.

Tabyrddau'r Babongo, Llandysul, Gwasg Gomer, 1961.

Y Blaned Dirion, Llandysul, Gwasg Gomer, 1968.

Y Gromlech yn yr Haidd, Llandysul, Gwasg Gomer, 1970.

Eira Mawr, Llandysul, Gwasg Gomer, 1971.

Harris, Llandysul, Gwasg Gomer, 1973.

Marwydos, Llandysul, Gwasg Gomer, 1974.

*Editor*

EDWARD TEGLA DAVIES: LLENOR A PHROFFWYD, Lerpwl, Gwasg y Brython, 1956.

STORÏAU'R DEFFRO, Caerdydd, Plaid Cymru, 1959.

TWENTY-FIVE WELSH SHORT STORIES (with Gwyn Jones), Oxford, Oxford University Press, 1971.

*Criticism and Biography*

'The Modern Novel in Welsh', in ANGLO-WELSH REVIEW (1958), XV/36, pp. 20–6.

Autobiographical Essay, in ARTISTS IN WALES (ed. Meic Stephens), Llandysul, Gwasg Gomer, 1971.

'Creu Ysgrif', in YSGRIFENNU CREADIGOL (ed. Geraint Bowen), Llandysul, Gwasg Gomer, 1972.

A selection of Islwyn Ffowc Elis's articles, essays and radio talks is published in NADDION (ed. Emlyn Evans), Dinbych, Gwasg Gee, 1998.

*Translations into English*

Stephens, Meic, SHADOW OF THE SICKLE, Llandysul, Gwasg Gomer, 1998.

Stephens, Meic, RETURN TO LLEIFIOR, Llandysul, Gwasg Gomer, 1999.

*Selected Criticism*

Brown, J. P., 'Islwyn Ffowc Elis', in ANGLO-WELSH REVIEW (1953), IX/24.

Pritchard, Marged, 'Islwyn Ffowc Elis', PORT-READAU'R FANER, Y Bala, Gwasg y Bala, 1976.

George, Delyth, ISLWYN FFOWC ELIS, Caernarfon, Gwasg Pantycelyn, 1990.

# *Acknowledgements*

I wish to thank Islwyn Ffowc Elis for his time and patience in answering my questions about his life and work, for his good-natured correspondence with me and for his hospitality during my time with him in Lampeter. I would also like to thank my wife, Susan, for her close, critical reading of the work in progress and her valuable suggestions on style. Finally, my thanks to Meic Stephens and R. Brinley Jones for reading the text in typescript and to Susan Jenkins and the staff at the University of Wales Press for maintaining their usual high standards in seeing this work through from first scribblings to print.

# *The Author*

T. Robin Chapman lives in Powys. In addition to part-time lecturing in the departments of Education and Welsh at University of Wales Aberystwyth, he is a freelance writer and translator.

*Designed by Jeff Clements*
*Typesetting at the University of Wales Press in*
*11pt Palatino and printed in Great Britain by*
*Dinefwr Press, Llandybïe, 2000*

© T. Robin Chapman, 2000

British Library Cataloguing in Publication Data.
A catalogue record for this book is available from the British Library.

ISBN 0-7083-1655-7

The Publishers wish to acknowledge the financial assistance of the Arts Council of Wales towards the cost of producing this volume.

The right of T. Robin Chapman to be identified as author of this work has been asserted by him in accordance with the Copyright, Designs and Patents Act 1988.

All rights reserved. No part of this book may be reproduced, stored in a retrieval system, or transmitted, in any form or by any means, electronic, mechanical, photocopying, recording or otherwise, without clearance from the University of Wales Press, 6 Gwennyth Street, Cardiff, CF24 4YD.
www.wales.ac.uk/press